Best of
Annie's *Signature* Designs:
Apparel

Paradiso Tunic, *page 40*

White Sand Tee, *page 45*

Cuyama Cardi, *page 26*

Table of Contents

Hoodie Cardigan

Design by Lena Skvagerson

SKILL LEVEL
Intermediate

FINISHED SIZES
Instructions given fit woman's size small; changes for medium, large, X-large, 2X-large and 3X-large are in [ ].

FINISHED MEASUREMENTS
Bust: 39½ inches *(small)* [42 inches *(medium)*, 47½ inches *(large)*, 51 inches *(X-large)*, 55½ inches *(2X-large)*, 58¼ inches *(3X-large)*]

Length: 28 inches *(small)* [28¾ inches *(medium)*, 29½ inches *(large)*, 30¼ inches *(X-large)*, 31 inches *(2X-large)*, 32 inches *(3X-large)*]

MATERIALS
- Plymouth Yarn Encore Worsted Tweed medium (worsted) weight acrylic/wool/rayon yarn (3½ oz/200 yds/100g per skein): 9 [10, 12, 13, 14, 15] skeins #T456 spiced pumpkin
- Size J/10/6mm crochet hook or size needed to obtain gauge
- Stitch markers: 7
- Tapestry needle

GAUGE
Working in pattern: 12 sts = 4 inches; 12 rows = 4 inches

Take time to check gauge.

PATTERN NOTES
Weave in loose ends as work progresses.

Skipped chains at beginning of row 1 count as first double crochet.

Chain-3 at beginning of row counts as first double crochet unless otherwise stated.

CARDIGAN
BACK
Row 1: Loosely ch 59 [65, 71, 77, 83, 87], dc in **4th ch from hook** *(see Pattern Notes)* and in each rem ch across, turn. *(57 [63, 69, 75, 81, 85] dc)*

Row 2 (RS): Ch 3 *(see Pattern Notes)*, ***fpdc** *(see Stitch Guide)* around next st, dc in next st; rep from * across, turn.

Row 3: Ch 3, ***bpdc** *(see Stitch Guide)* around next st, dc in next st; rep from * across, turn.

Rep rows 2 and 3 until piece measures 19½ [20, 20½, 20¾, 21¼, 22] inches.

Place a marker on each side to mark beg of armhole.

Work even until piece measures 28 [28¾, 29½, 30¼, 31, 32] inches, ending with a WS row.

Fasten off.

LEFT FRONT
Row 1: Loosely ch 33 [35, 39, 41, 45, 47], dc in 4th ch from hook and in rem each ch across, turn. *(31 [33, 37, 39, 43, 45] dc)*

Row 2 (RS): Ch 3, *fpdc around next st, dc in next st; rep from * across to last 2 dc, dc in last 2 dc, turn.

Row 3: Ch 3, dc in next 2 dc, *bpdc around next st, dc in next st; rep from * across, turn.

Rep rows 2 and 3 until piece measures 19½ [20, 20½, 20¾, 21¼, 22] inches.

Place a marker on each side to mark beg of armhole.

Work even until piece measures 28 [28¾, 29½, 30¼, 31, 32] inches, ending with a WS row.

Fasten off.

RIGHT FRONT
Row 1: Loosely ch 33 [35, 39, 41, 45, 47], dc in 4th ch from hook and in each rem ch across, turn. *(31 [33, 37, 39, 43, 45] dc)*

Row 2 (RS): Ch 3, dc in next 2 dc, *fpdc around next st, dc in next st; rep from * across, turn.

Row 3: Ch 3, *bpdc around next st, dc in next st; rep from * across to last 2 dc, dc in last 2 dc, turn.

Rep rows 2 and 3 until piece measures 19½ [20, 20½, 20¾, 21¼, 22] inches.

Place a marker on each side to mark beg of armhole.

Work even until piece measures 28 [28¾, 29½, 30¼, 31, 32] inches, ending with a WS row.

Do not fasten off.

SLEEVE
Make 2.

Cuff
Row 1: Loosely ch 35 [37, 37, 39, 39, 41], dc in 4th ch from hook and in each rem ch across, turn. *(33 [35, 35, 37, 37, 39] dc)*

Row 2 (WS): Ch 3, *fpdc around next st, dc in next st; rep from * across, turn.

Row 3: Ch 3, *bpdc around next st, dc in next st, rep from * across, turn.

Rep rows 2 and 3 until piece measures 3 [3, 3½, 3½, 4, 4] inches, ending with a RS row.

Arm
Set-up row (WS): Rep row 3.

Note: Place a marker at beg of next row and measure from here.

Row 1 (RS): Ch 3, *fpdc around next st, dc in next st; rep from * across, turn.

Row 2: Ch 3, *bpdc around next st, dc in next st; rep from * across, turn.

Rep rows 1 and 2 until piece measures 3 [3, 3½, 3½, 4, 4] inches from marker, ending with a WS row.

Inc row: Ch 3, dc in st at base of ch, work in established pattern to last st, 2 dc in last st, turn. *(35 [37, 37, 39, 39, 41] dc)*

Continue even in established pattern, working an increase row every 4th [4th, 3rd, 3rd, 3rd, 3rd] row 8 [8, 9, 9, 10, 10] times. *(51 [53, 55, 57, 59, 61] dc after last inc row)*

Work even until piece measures 17 [17, 17½, 17½, 17½, 18] inches from marker, ending with a WS row.

Sleeve Cap

Row 1 (RS): Ch 1, sl st in first 4 sts, ch 1, sc in next st, work across in established pattern to last 6 sts, dc in next st, sc in next st, turn, leaving rem 4 sts unworked. *(43 [45, 47, 49, 51, 53] sts)*

Rows 2–4: Rep row 1. *(19 [21, 23, 25, 27, 29] sts after row 4)*

Fasten off.

POCKET

Make 2.

Row 1: Loosely ch 25 [25, 25, 27, 27, 27], dc in 4th ch from hook and in each rem ch across, turn. *(23 [23, 23, 25, 25, 25] dc)*

Row 2 (RS): Ch 3, *fpdc around next st, dc in next st; rep from * across, turn.

Row 3: Ch 3, *bpdc around next st, dc in next st; rep from * across, turn.

Rep rows 2 and 3 until piece measures 6½ [6½, 7, 7, 7½, 7½] inches, ending with a RS row.

Last row: Ch 1, sc in each st across. Fasten off.

ASSEMBLY

With WS tog, sew side seams up to markers.

Sew shoulder seams 6½ [6¾, 8, 9, 9½, 10] inches from outer edge toward neck opening.

HOOD

Starting at the upper corner to work toward neck, return live lp from Right Front to hook.

Row 1 (RS): Ch 1, work 45 [45, 49, 49, 53, 53] sc evenly around neck opening, turn.

Row 2: Ch 3, *2 dc in next st, dc in next st; rep from * across, turn. *(67 [67, 73, 73, 79, 79] dc)*

Row 3: Ch 3, dc in next 2 dc, *fpdc around next st, dc in next st; rep from * across to last 2 dc, dc in last 2 dc, turn.

Row 4: Ch 3, dc in next 2 dc, *bpdc around next st, dc in next st; rep from * across to last 2 dc, dc in last 2 dc, turn.

Rep rows 3 and 4 until piece measures 14 [14½, 14½, 15, 15, 15½] inches. Fasten off.

Fold Hood double and sew tog at top.

FINISHING

Sew Sleeve seams. Matching top fold of sleeve to shoulder seam, sew Sleeves into armhole openings.

Sew a Pocket to each Front, positioning each Pocket approximately 2 to 2½ inches from Front edge and 2 to 2½ inches above bottom edge. Fold up Cuffs. Weave in ends. ●

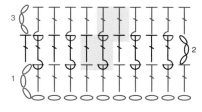

STITCH KEY
- Chain (ch)
- Double crochet (dc)
- Front post double crochet (fpdc)
- Back post double crochet (bpdc)

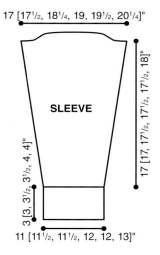

Hoodie Cardigan
Stitch Diagram
Note: Reps shown in gray.

17 [17½, 18¼, 19, 19½, 20¼]"

17 [17, 17½, 17½, 17½, 18]"

SLEEVE

3 [3, 3½, 3½, 4, 4]"

11 [11½, 11½, 12, 12, 13]"

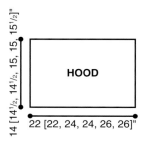

14 [14½, 14½, 15, 15, 15½]"

HOOD

22 [22, 24, 24, 26, 26]"

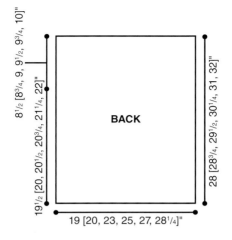

8½ [8¾, 9, 9½, 9¾, 10]"

19½ [20, 20½, 20¾, 21¼, 22]"

28 [28¾, 29½, 30¼, 31, 32]"

BACK

19 [20, 23, 25, 27, 28¼]"

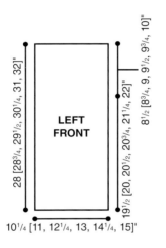

28 [28¾, 29½, 30¼, 31, 32]"

19½ [20, 20½, 20¾, 21¼, 22]"

8½ [8¾, 9, 9½, 9¾, 10]"

LEFT FRONT

10¼ [11, 12¼, 13, 14¼, 15]"

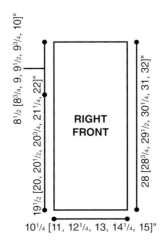

8½ [8¾, 9, 9½, 9¾, 10]"

19½ [20, 20½, 20¾, 21¼, 22]"

28 [28¾, 29½, 30¼, 31, 32]"

RIGHT FRONT

10¼ [11, 12¼, 13, 14¼, 15]"

Euphoria Cardi

Design by Lena Skvagerson

SKILL LEVEL
Intermediate

FINISHED SIZES
Instructions are given to fit woman's size small; changes for medium, large, X-large, 2X-large and 3X-large are in [ ].

FINISHED MEASUREMENTS
From shoulder to shoulder: 14 inches *(small)* [15 inches *(medium)*, 16 inches *(large)*, 17 inches *(X-large)*, 18 inches *(2X-large)*, 19 inches *(3X-large)*]

Length in back: 21½ inches *(small)* [22½ inches *(medium)*, 23½ inches *(large)*, 24½ inches *(X-large)*, 25½ inches *(2X-large)*, 26½ inches *(3X-large)*] *(measure from top of Armhole to bottom edge)*

MATERIALS
- Lion Brand Yarn Mandala light (DK) weight acrylic yarn (5⅓ oz/590 yds/150g per ball): 4 [4, 4, 4, 5, 5] balls #214 centaur
- Or use: Lion Brand Yarn Vanna's Style light (DK) weight acrylic yarn (3½ oz/254 yds/100g per ball): 8 [8, 9, 9, 10, 10] balls #124 camel
- Or use: King Cole Riot DK light (DK) weight acrylic/wool yarn (3½ oz/324 yds/100g per skein): 5 [5, 6, 6, 7, 8] skeins #405 urban
- Size J/10/6mm crochet hook or size needed to obtain gauge
- Tapestry needle

GAUGE
13 dc = 4 inches; 6¾ dc rows = 4 inches

Take time to check gauge.

PATTERN NOTES
Weave in loose ends as work progresses.

Chain-3 at beginning of round counts as first double crochet unless otherwise stated.

Chain-2 at beginning of round counts as first half-double crochet unless otherwise stated.

Join with slip stitch as indicated unless otherwise stated.

SPECIAL STITCHES
Puff stitch (PS): [Yo, insert hook in indicated st, yo and pull up a lp matching the height of a dc] twice *(5 lps on hook)*, yo, draw through all lps on hook, ch 1.

Front post treble 2 stitches together (FPtr2tog): Yo twice, insert hook around post of first indicated st from front around back and out to front, yo, pull up a lp, [yo, draw through 2 lps] twice, yo twice, insert hook around post 2nd indicated st from front, yo, pull up a lp, [yo, draw through 2 lps] twice, yo, draw through all lps on hook.

CARDI
BACK
Ch 4, **join** *(see Pattern Notes)* in first ch to form ring.

Rnd 1: Ch 3 *(see Pattern Notes)*, work [**PS**—*see Special Stitches,* ch 1] 4 times in ring, join in top of first PS at beg of rnd. *(4 PS)*

Rnd 2: Ch 2 *(see Pattern Notes)*, [5 dc in sp before next PS, hdc in ch above next PS] 3 times, 5 dc in sp before PS at beg of rnd 1, join in top of beg ch-2. *(20 dc, 4 hdc)*

Rnd 3: Ch 1, sc in same st, sc in next 2 sts, 3 sc in next dc *(corner made)*, [sc in next 5 sts, 3 sc in next dc *(corner made)*] 3 times, sc in next 2 sts, join in first sc at beg of rnd. *(32 sc)*

Rnd 4: Ch 1, sc in same st, sc in next sc, work **FPtr2tog** *(see Special Stitches)* around (first hdc and center corner dc) 2 rnds below, sk 1 sc on working row, sc in next sc, [1 dc in next sc *(corner)*, 1 sc in in next sc, work FPtr2tog around (same center corner dc and next hdc) 2 rnds below, sk 1 sc on working row**, sc in next 3 sc, work FPtr2tog around (same hdc and next center corner dc) 2 rnds below, sk 1 sc on working row, sc in next sc] around, ending final rep at **, 1 sc in last sc, join in first sc at beg of rnd. *(32 sts)*

Rnd 5: Ch 1, sc in same st, sc in next 3 sts, 3 sc in next corner dc, [sc in next 7 sts, 3 sc in next corner dc] 3 times, sc in last 3 sts, join in first sc at beg of rnd. *(40 sc)*

Rnd 6: Ch 1, sc in same st, sc in next sc, **fpdc** *(see Stitch Guide)* around next FPtr2tog 2 rows below, sk 1 sc on working row, sc in next 2 sts, 3 sc in next sc *(corner)*, [sc in next 2 sc, fpdc around next FPtr2tog 2 rows below, sk 1 sc on working row, sc in next 3 sc, fpdc around next FPtr2tog 2 rows below, sk 1 sc on working row, sc in next 2 sts, 3 sc in next sc *(corner)*] 3 times, sc in next 2 sc, fpdc around next FPtr2tog 2 rows below, sk 1 sc on working row, sc in last sc, join in first sc at beg of rnd. *(48 sts)*

Rnd 7: Sl st in next 2 sts, ch 3, 2 dc in fpdc, ch 1, sk 2 sts, 3 dc in next sc, [ch 3, sk 1 sc in corner, 3 dc in next sc, ch 1, sk next 2 sts, 3 dc in next fpdc, ch 1, sk next 3 sts, 3 dc in next fpdc, ch 1, sk next 2 sts, 3 dc in next sc] 3 times, ch 3, sk 1 sc in corner, 3 dc in next sc, ch 1, sk next 2 sts, 3 dc in next fpdc, ch 1, join in top of beg ch-3. *(48 dc, 12 ch-1 sps, 4 ch-3 sps)*

Rnd 8: Ch 3, [1 dc in each dc and around each ch across to ch-3 sp in corner, in ch-3 sp work (2 dc, ch 3, 2 dc)] 4 times, 1 dc in each dc and around each ch across, join in top of beg ch-3. *(76 dc, 4 ch-3 sps)*

Rnd 9: Sl st in next dc, ch 3, 2 dc in same dc, ch 1, sk next 3 sts, [3 dc in next st, ch 1, sk next 3 sts] across to corner, [(3 dc, ch 3, 3 dc) in next corner ch sp, {ch 1, sk next 3 sts, 3 dc in next dc} across to last 3 dc before next corner, ch 1, sk next 3 sts] around, ending at first 3-dc group, ch 1, join in top of beg ch-3.

Rep rnds 8 and 9 until square measures approximately 14 [15, 16, 17, 18, 19] inches across, ending with rnd 8.

ARMHOLES

Next rnd: Sl st in next dc, ch 3, 2 dc in same dc, ch 1, sk next 3 sts, [3 dc in next st, ch 1, sk next 3 sts] across to corner, (3 dc, ch 3, 2 dc) in next corner ch-3 sp, ch 22 [22, 26, 26, 30, 30], sk next 23 [23, 27, 27, 31, 31] sts, [[3 dc in next dc, ch 1, sk next 3 sts} across to corner, (3 dc, ch 3, 3 dc) in next corner ch sp, ch 1, sk next 3 sts] twice, [3 dc in next dc, ch 1, sk next 3 sts] across to last 24 [24, 28, 28, 32, 32] dc before next corner, 3 dc in next dc, ch 22 [22, 26, 26, 30, 30], sk next 23 [23, 27, 27, 31, 31] sts, (2 dc, ch 3, 3 dc) in next corner ch sp, [ch 1, sk next 3 sts, 3 dc in next dc] across to last 3 dc on rnd, ch 1, join in top of beg ch-3.

Next rnd: Rep rnd 8 working a dc into each ch of Armhole ch.

Next rnd: Rep rnd 9.

Next 8 rnds: [Rep rnds 8 an 9] 4 times.

Square measures approximately 26 [27, 28, 29, 30, 31] inches.

Fasten off.

LEFT FRONT

Now working in rows, with RS facing, join in upper corner ch-3 sp to work along edge parallel to Armhole.

Row 1 (RS): Ch 3, dc in ch-3 sp, dc in each dc and ch sp across to corner, 2 dc in corner ch sp, turn.

Row 2: Ch 4, sk next 2 sts, [3 dc in next dc, ch 1, sk next 3 sts] across to last 4 sts, 3 dc in next dc, ch 1, sk next 2 sts, dc in top of beg ch-3, turn.

Row 3: Ch 3, dc in first ch sp, dc in each dc and ch sp across to last ch sp, dc in last ch sp, dc in top of beg ch-3, turn.

Rep [rows 2 and 3] until Left Front measures approximately 14½ [15, 15½, 16, 16½, 17] inches from Armhole, ending with a RS row.

Left Front Edge

Row 1 (WS): Ch 2, [**bpdc** *(see Stitch Guide)* in next dc, fpdc in next dc] across to last 2 sts, bpdc in next dc, hdc in top of beg ch-3.

Row 2: Ch 2, [fpdc in next st, bpdc in next st] across to last 2 sts, fpdc in next st, hdc in top of beg ch-2.

Row 3: Ch 2, [bpdc in next st, fpdc in next st] across to last 2 sts, bpdc in next st, hdc in top of beg ch-2.

Row 4: Rep row 2.

Fasten off.

RIGHT FRONT

With RS facing and orienting work to crochet across opposite edge parallel to Armhole, join in ch-3 sp in lower corner and work as Left Front and Left Front Edge.

EDGES

Top Front

Work along upper edge of body. Join in st at upper corner of Right Front.

Row 1 (RS): Ch 3, work 1 dc in each st along upper edge, and evenly along the short ends of front bands, making sure to get an odd number of sts, turn.

Rows 2–5: Work as rows 1–4 on Left Front Edge.

Fasten off.

Lower Front

Working along bottom edge of body. Join in st at lower corner of Left Front and work as for rows 1–5 of Top Front Edge.

Fasten off.

SLEEVES

Rnd 1: Join at the bottom of Armhole, ch 3, work 22 [22, 26, 26, 30, 30] dc evenly along edge up to top of Armhole, 1 dc at top, 22 [22, 26, 26, 30, 30] dc evenly along edge down to bottom of Armhole, join in top of beg ch-3. *(46 [46, 54, 54, 62, 62] dc)*

Rnd 2 (dec): Ch 3, **dc dec** *(see Stitch Guide)* in next 2 dc, dc in each dc around to last 2 dc, dc dec in last 2 dc, join in top of beg ch-3. *(44 [44, 52, 52, 60, 60] dc)*

Rnd 3: Ch 3, working in **back lps** *(see Stitch Guide)* around, dc in next 7 [7, 12, 12, 16, 16] dc, place marker in last st, ch 1, sk next 2 sts [3 dc in next dc, ch 1, sk next 3 sts] 6 times, 3 dc in next dc, ch 1, sk next 2 sts, dc in each dc to end, join in top of beg ch-3. Move marker up as rnds are worked.

Rnd 4: Ch 3, working in both lps, dc in each dc and ch sp around, join in top of beg ch-3.

Rnd 5: Ch 3, working in back lps around, dc in each dc across to and including st with marker, ch 1, sk next

2 sts, [3 dc in next dc, ch 1, sk next 3 sts] 6 times, 3 dc in next dc, ch 1, sk next 2 sts, dc in each dc to end, join in top of beg ch-3.

Rnd 6 (dec): Ch 3, working in both lps, dc dec in next 2 dc, dc in each dc and ch-sp around to last 2 dc, dc dec in last 2 dc, join in 3rd ch at beg of rnd. *(42 [42, 50, 50, 58, 58] dc)*

Rnd 7: Rep rnd 5.

Rnd 8: Rep rnd 4.

Rnd 9: Rep rnd 5.

Rnd 10 (dec): Rep rnd 6. *(40 [40, 48, 48, 56, 56] dc)*

Continue in established pattern, rep dec rnd on every 4th [4th, 4th, 4th, 3rd, 3rd] rnd until 34 [34, 40, 40, 44, 44] dc rem on rnd.

Continue in established pattern without dec until Sleeve measures 16½ [17, 17½, 18, 18½, 19] inches, ending with a dc in each dc around.

Cuff

Rnd 1: Ch 3, [fpdc in next dc, dc in next dc] around to last dc, fpdc in last dc, join in top of beg ch-3.

Rnds 2–4: Ch 3, [fpdc in next fpdc, dc in next dc] around to last fpdc, fpdc in last fpdc, join in top of beg ch-3.

Fasten off. ●

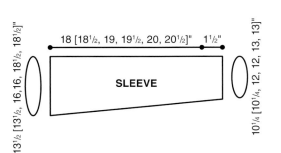

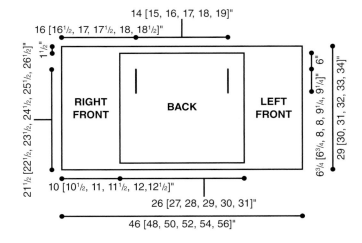

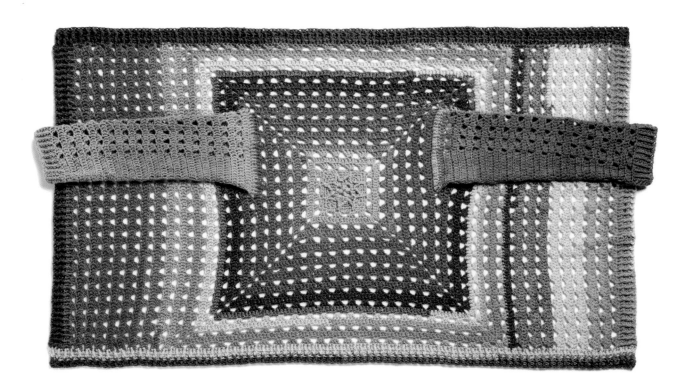

Exeter Gansey Cardigan

Design by Melissa Leapman

SKILL LEVEL

Intermediate

FINISHED SIZES

Instructions given fit size small; changes for medium, large, X-large and 2X-large are in parentheses.

FINISHED MEASUREMENTS

Bust: 43 inches (47 inches, 51 inches, 55 inches, 59 inches)

Length: 32 inches (32 inches, 32½ inches, 32½ inches, 33 inches)

MATERIALS

- King Cole Majestic DK light (DK) weight superwash wool/ acrylic/polyamide yarn (1¾ oz/131 yds/50g per ball): 26 (27, 29, 30, 31) balls amber #2658
- Size H/8/5mm crochet hook or size needed to obtain gauge
- Size J/10/6mm crochet hook or size needed to obtain gauge
- Tapestry needle

GAUGE

In Pattern Stitch: 16 sts = 4 inches; 21 rows = 4 inches

Take time to check gauge.

PATTERN NOTES

Chain-3 at end of row counts as first double crochet of next row unless otherwise stated.

Chain-2 at end of row counts as first half double crochet of next row unless otherwise stated.

Chain-1 at end of row does not count as a stitch unless otherwise stated.

SPECIAL STITCH

Popcorn (pc): 5 dc into the indicated st; drop the lp from the hook; reinsert the hook into the first dc of the 5-dc group, pick up the dropped lp and pull it through the first dc.

PATTERN STITCH

Textured Pattern (multiple of 4 + 2 sts)
Basketweave Section

Foundation row (WS): Dc into the 4th ch from the hook *(sk ch counts as dc)* and into each ch across. **Ch 2** *(see Pattern Notes)*, turn.

Row 1 (RS): [**Bpdc** *(see Stitch Guide)* around the next 2 sts, **fpdc** *(see Stitch Guide)* around the next 2 sts] across, ending with hdc into the top of the turning ch. Ch 2, turn.

Row 2: Rep row 1.

Row 3: [Fpdc around the next 2 sts, bpdc around the next 2 sts] across, ending with hdc into the top of the turning ch-2. Ch 2, turn.

Row 4: Rep row 3.

Rows 5–8: Rep rows 1–4 once more. At end of last row, **ch 3** *(see Pattern Notes)*, turn.

Row 9 (RS): Dc into each st across. Ch 1, **do not turn.**

Row 10: Working from left to right, **reverse sc** *(see Stitch Guide)* into the **front lp** *(see Stitch Guide)* only of each st across. **Ch 1** *(see Pattern Notes)*, **do not turn.**

Textured Lattice Section

Row 11: Working in unused **back lps** *(see Stitch Guide)* of row 9, sc into each st across. Ch 1, turn.

Rows 12–14: Sc into each st across. Ch 1, turn.

Row 15: Sc into the first 2 sc, **fptr** *(see Stitch Guide)* around the 2nd sc 3 rows below, *sk the next 2 sc 3 rows below, fptr around the next sc 3 rows below, on current row sc into the next 2 sc**, fptr around the sc to the left of the last fptr made 3 rows below, rep from * across, ending last rep at **. Ch 1, turn.

Rows 16–18: Rep row 12.

Row 19: Sc into the first sc, [sk the first 2 sc 3 rows below, fptr around the next sc 3 rows below, on current row sc into the next 2 sc, fptr around the sc to the left of the last fptr made 3 rows below] across, sc into the last sc. Ch 1, turn.

Rows 20 & 21: Sc into each st across. Ch 1, turn. At end of last row, **do not turn.**

Row 22: Rep row 10. Ch 1, **do not turn.**

Popcorn Section

Row 23: Rep row 11.

Row 24: Sc in each st across. Ch 1, turn.

Row 25: Sc in the first 2 sts, [**pc** *(see Special Stitch)* in next st, sc in next 3 sts] across. Ch 1, turn.

Rows 26 & 27: Sc into each st across. After row 26, ch 1, turn. After row 27, ch 1, **do not turn.**

Row 28: Rep row 10.

Row 29: Sl st in unused back lps of row 27 across. Ch 3, turn.

Row 30: Dc into each st across. Ch 2, turn.

Rep rows 1–30 for pattern.

CARDIGAN

BACK

With the smaller hook, ch 88 (96, 104, 112, 120).

Beg the **Textured Pattern** *(see Pattern Stitch)*, and work even on 86 (94, 102, 110, 118) sts until the piece measures approximately 24 inches from beg, ending after a rep of row 20 of pattern. Do not ch after last row. Turn.

Shape Armholes

Next row (RS): Sl st into the first 5 (5, 9, 9, 9) sts, ch 1, work the pattern as established to the last 4 (4, 8, 8, 8) sts. Ch 1, **do not turn**, leaving the rest of the row unworked. *[78 (86, 86, 94, 102) sts]*

Continue even in the pattern as established until the piece measures approximately 32 (32, 32½, 32½, 33) inches from beg, ending after a WS row.

Fasten off.

LEFT FRONT

With the smaller hook, ch 32 (36, 40, 44, 48).

Beg the Textured Pattern, and work even on 30 (34, 38, 42, 46) sts until the piece measures approximately 24 inches from beg, ending after a rep of row 20 of pattern. Do not ch after last row. Turn.

Shape Armhole

Next row (RS): Sl st into the first 5 (5, 9, 9, 9) sts, ch 1, work to end the row. Ch 1, **do not turn**, leaving the rest of the row unworked. *[26 (30, 30, 34, 38) sts]*

Continue even in the pattern as established until the piece measures approximately 32 (32, 32½, 32½, 33) inches from beg, ending after a WS row.

Fasten off.

RIGHT FRONT

With the smaller hook, ch 32 (36, 40, 44, 48).

Beg the Textured Pattern, and work even on 30 (34, 38, 42, 46) sts until the piece measures approximately 24 inches from beg, ending after a rep of row 20 of pattern. Do not ch after last row. Turn.

Shape Armhole

Next row (RS): Work across in Textured Pattern until 4 (4, 8, 8, 8) sts rem. Ch 1, **do not turn**, leaving the rest of the row unworked. *[26 (30, 30, 34, 38) sts]*

Continue even in the pattern as established until the piece measures the same as the Left Front, ending after a WS row.

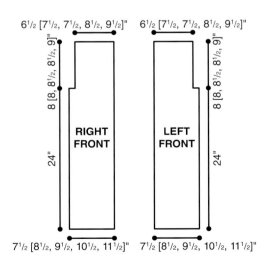

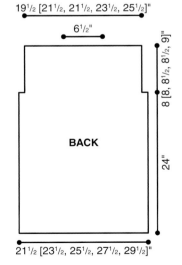

SLEEVES

With the smaller hook, ch 36.

Beg the Textured Pattern on 34 sts, and work even for 2 inches.

Continue the pattern as established, inc 1 st each side every row 0 (0, 0, 0, 6) times, every 4 rows 5 (6, 14, 16, 13) times, then every 6 rows 10 (9, 3, 1, 0) time(s), working new sts into the pattern as they accumulate. [64 (64, 68, 68, 72) sts]

Continue even until the piece measures approximately 18¾ (18¼, 18¼, 17¼, 16¾) inches from beg, ending after a WS row.

Fasten off.

FINISHING

Sew the shoulder seams, leaving the center 26 sts unsewn for the back of the neck.

Front Bands

With the RS facing and the larger hook, join yarn with sl st to the lower right front edge and ch 2.

Row 1: Work a total of 257 (257, 259, 259, 261) hdc evenly along the right front, around the neck and down the left front. Ch 2, turn.

Row 2: Hdc in back lps only across. Ch 2, turn.

Rep row 2 until the front bands measure approximately 11 inches.

Fasten off. ●

16 [16, 17, 17, 18]"

SLEEVE

18¾ [18¼, 18¼, 17¼, 16¾]"

8½"

Harbor Lights Circle Jacket

Design by Lena Skvagerson

SKILL LEVEL
Intermediate

FINISHED SIZES
Instructions given fit size small/medium, changes for large/X-large and 2X-large/3X-large are in [ ].

When only 1 number is given, it applies to all sizes.

FINISHED MEASUREMENTS
Cross Back: 12½ inches *(small/medium)* [13½ inches *(large/X-large)*, 14½ inches *(2X-large/3X-large)*]

Length: Approximately 30¾ inches *(small/medium)* [35 inches *(large/X-large)*, 39¼ inches *(2X-large/3X-large)*]

Diameter: Approximately 35 inches *(small/medium)* [41 inches *(large/X-large)*, 46½ inches *(2X-large/3X-large)*]

MATERIALS
- Universal Yarn Classic Shades Frenzy bulky (chunky) weight acrylic/wool yarn (3½ oz/158 yds/100g per ball):

  5
  BULKY

    5 [7, 8] balls #905 harbor lights
- Size K/10½/6.5mm crochet hook or size needed to obtain gauge
- Tapestry needle
- Stitch marker

GAUGE
11 dc = 4 inches; 7 dc rows = 4 inches

Take time to check gauge.

PATTERN NOTES
Weave in loose ends as work progresses.

Join with slip stitch as indicated unless otherwise stated.

Chain-3 at beginning of round counts as first double crochet unless otherwise stated.

Chain-5 at beginning of round counts as first double crochet and chain-2 unless otherwise stated.

Chain-4 at beginning of round counts as first treble crochet unless otherwise stated.

JACKET
Rnd 1: Ch 4, join *(see Pattern Notes)* in first ch to form ring, ch 3, 11 dc in ring, join in top of beg ch-3. *(12 dc)*

Place marker to indicate beg of rnd.

Rnd 2: Ch 3 *(see Pattern Notes)*, dc in st at base of ch-3, 2 dc in each st around, join in top of beg ch-3. *(24 dc)*

Rnd 3: Ch 3, 2 dc in next dc, [dc in next dc, 2 dc in next dc] around, join in top of beg ch-3. *(36 dc)*

Rnd 4: Ch 3, dc in next dc, 2 dc in next dc, [dc in next 2 dc, 2 dc in next dc] around, join in top of beg ch-3. *(48 dc)*

Rnd 5: Ch 5 *(see Pattern Notes)*, sk next dc, dc in next dc, ch 2, [sk next dc, dc in next dc, ch 2] around, join in 3rd ch of beg ch-5. *(24 dc, 24 ch-2 sps)*

Rnd 6: Ch 4 *(see Pattern Notes)*, 2 tr in st at base of beg ch-4, [ch 3, sk next 2 ch sps, 3 tr in next dc] around, end with ch 3, sk last 2 ch sps, join in top of beg ch-4. *(12 3-tr groups, 12 ch-3 sps)*

Rnd 7: Ch 3, dc in next 2 tr, 5 dc in next ch-3 sp, [dc in next 3 tr, 5 dc in next ch-3 sp] around, join in top of beg ch-3. *(96 dc)*

Rnd 8: Rep rnd 5. *(48 dc, 48 ch-2 sps)*

Rnd 9: Ch 4, 2 tr in st at base of beg ch-4, [ch 3, sk next 3 ch sps, 3 tr in next dc] around, end with ch 3, sk last 3 ch sps, join in top of beg ch-4. *(16 3-tr groups, 16 ch-3 sps)*

Rnd 10: Rep rnd 7. *(128 dc)*

Note: *At this point, diameter = 14 inches; circumference = 44 inches.*

Rnd 11: Rep rnd 5. *(64 dc, 64 ch-2 sps)*

Rnd 12: Ch 4, 2 tr in st at base of beg ch-4, [ch 3, sk next 3 ch sps, 3 tr in next dc] 4 times, [ch 3, sk next 2 ch sps, 3 tr in next dc] 2 times, ch 3, *[sk next 3 ch sps, 3 tr in next dc, ch 3] 4 times, [sk next 2 ch sps, 3 tr in next dc, ch 3] 2 times, rep from * once, [sk next 3 ch sps, 3 tr in next dc, ch 3] 4 times, sk next 2 ch sps, 3 tr in next dc, ch 3, sk next 2 ch sps, join in top of beg ch-4. *(24 3-tr groups, 24 ch-3 sps)*

Rnd 13: Ch 3, dc in next 2 tr, 4 dc in next ch-3 sp, [dc in next 3 tr, 4 dc in next ch-3 sp] around, join in top of beg ch-3. *(168 dc)*

Note: *Diameter = 18½ inches; circumference = 58 inches.*

Size Large/X-Large Only

Rnd [14]: Ch 4 *(counts as first dc and ch-1)*, sk next dc, [dc in next dc, ch 1, sk next dc] around, join in 3rd ch of beg ch-4. *([84 dc, 84 ch sps])*

Rnd [15]: Ch 3, dc in st at base of beg ch-3, dc in next 11 sts, [2 dc in next dc, 1 dc in next 11 sts] around, join in top of beg ch-3. *([182 dc])*

Rnd [16]: Ch 3, dc in same st as beg ch-3, dc in next 12 sts, [2 dc in next dc, 1 dc in next 12 sts] around, join in top of beg ch-3. ([196 dc])

Note: Diameter = 22 inches; circumference = 69 inches.

Size 2X-Large/3X-Large Only

Rnd [14]: Rep rnd 5. ([84 dc, 84 ch-2 sps])

Rnd [15]: Ch 4, 2 tr in st at base of beg ch-4, [ch 3, sk next 3 ch sps, 3 tr in next dc] around, end with ch 3, sk last 3 ch sps, join in top of beg ch-4. ([28 3-tr groups, 28 ch-3 sps])

Rnd [16]: Rep rnd 13. ([196 dc])

Rnd [17]: Ch 3, dc in st at base of beg ch-3, dc in next 13 sts, [2 dc in next dc, dc in next 13 sts] around, join in top of beg ch-3. ([210 dc])

Rnd [18]: Ch 3, dc in st at base of beg ch-3, dc in next 20 sts, [2 dc in next dc, dc in next 20 sts] around, join in top of beg ch-3. ([220 dc])

Note: Diameter = 25½ inches; circumference = 80 inches.

ARMHOLE SHAPING All Sizes

Rnd 1: Ch 3, dc in next 17 [18, 19] dc, loosely ch 21 [24, 29], sk next 21 [23, 25] dc *(armhole made)*, dc in next 90 [112, 130] dc *(for back)*, loosely ch 21 [24, 29], sk next 21 [23, 25] dc *(armhole made)*, dc in next 18 [19, 20] dc, join in top of beg ch-3. *(168 [198, 228] sts)*

FRONT & COLLAR

Rnd 2: Ch 5, sk next st, dc in next st, [ch 2, sk next st, dc in next st] around, join in top of 3rd ch of beg ch-5. *(84 [99, 114] dc, 84 [99, 114] ch-2 sps)*

Rnd 3: Ch 4, 2 tr in same st as beg ch-4, [ch 3, sk next 3 ch sps, 3 tr in next dc] around, end with ch 3, sk last 3 ch sps,

join in top of beg ch-4. *(28 [33, 38] 3-tr groups, 28 [33, 38] ch-3 sps)*

Rnd 4: Ch 3, dc in next 2 tr, 4 [5, 4] dc in next ch-3 sp, [dc in next 3 tr, 5 dc in next ch-3 sp, dc in next 3 tr, 4 dc in next ch-3 sp] around until 1 [0, 1] ch-3 sp(s) rem, dc in next 3 tr, 5 [0, 4] dc in last ch-3 sp, join in top of beg ch-3. *(210 [248, 284] dc)*

Rnd 5: Ch 4, sk next dc, [dc in next dc, ch 1, sk next dc] around, join in top of beg ch-4. *(105 [124, 142] dc, 105 [124, 142] ch sps)*

Rnd 6: Ch 3, 1 dc in st at base of beg ch-3, dc in next 9 [14, 34] sts, [2 dc in next st, 1 dc in next 8 [14, 34] sts] around to last 11 [8, 4] sts, dc in each st to end of rnd, join in top of beg ch-3. *(232 [264, 292] dc)*

Rnd 7: Rep rnd 5.

Rnd 8: Ch 3, dc in st at base of beg ch-3, dc in next 10 [8, 6] sts, [2 dc in next st, dc in next 12 {14, 14} sts] around, join in top of beg ch-3. *(250 [282, 312] dc)*

Rnd 9: Rep rnd 5.

Rnd 10: Ch 3, dc in st at base of beg ch-3, dc in next 2 [9, 17] sts, [2 dc in next st, dc in next 12 {15, 13} sts] around, join in top of beg ch-3. *(270 [300, 334] dc)*

Rnd 11: Rep rnd 5.

Rnd 12: Ch 3, dc in st at base of beg ch-3, dc in next 3 [14, 10] sts, [2 dc in next st, dc in next 13 {14, 18} sts] around, join in top of beg ch-3. *(290 [320, 352] dc)*

Note: *Diameter = 33½ [37, 40½] inches; circumference = 105½ [116½, 127½] inches; Front from Armhole opening measures approximately 7½ inches.*

Size Small/Medium Only

Rnd 13: Ch 3, dc in st at base of beg ch-3, dc in next 28 dc, [2 dc in next dc, dc in next 28 dc] around, join in top of beg ch-3. Fasten off. *(300 dc)*

Note: *Front from Armhole opening measures approximately 8¼ inches.*

Sizes Large/X-Large & 2X-Large/3X-Large Only

Rnd [13]: Rep rnd 5.

Rnd [14]: Ch 3, dc in st at base of beg ch-3, dc in next [15, 9] sts, [2 dc in next st, dc in next {15, 17} sts] around. *([340, 372] dc)*

Note: *Diameter = [39½, 43] inches; circumference = [124, 134¾] inches.*

Size Large/X-Large Only

Rnd [15]: Ch 3, dc in st at base of beg ch-3, dc in next 33 dc, [2 dc in next dc, dc in next 33 dc] around, join in top of beg ch-3. Fasten off. *([350] dc)*

Note: *Front from Armhole opening measures approximately 9½ inches.*

Size 2X-Large/3X-Large Only

Rnd [15]: Rep rnd 5.

Rnd [16]: Ch 3, dc in st at base of beg ch-3, dc in next [14] sts, [2 dc in next st, dc in next {20} sts] around. *([390] dc)*

Rnd [17]: Ch 3, dc in st at base of beg ch-3, dc in next 38 dc, [2 dc in next dc, dc in next 38 dc] around, join in top of beg ch-3. Fasten off. *([400] dc)*

Note: *Front from Armhole opening measures approximately 10½ inches.*

SLEEVE

Make 2.

Rnd 1: Beg at bottom of first Armhole opening, join in side of dc at bottom, ch 3, dc in each dc up to top of Armhole, 1 [2, 1] dc in side of dc at top, dc in each dc and ch sp to end of rnd, join in top of beg ch-3. *(44 [50, 56] dc)*

Rnd 2: Ch 3, dc in each dc around, join in top of beg ch-3.

Rnd 3: Ch 3, **dc dec** *(see Stitch Guide)* in next 2 dc, dc in each dc around to last 2 dc, dc dec in last 2 dc, join in top of beg ch-3. *(42 [48, 54] dc)*

Rnds 4–17 [4–21, 4–25]: [Rep rnds 2 and 3] 7 [9, 11] times. *(28 [30, 32] dc)*

Rep rnd 2 until Sleeve measures 13 [13½, 14½] inches.

Cuff

Rnd 1: Ch 4, sk next dc, [dc in next dc, ch 1, sk next dc] around, join in 3rd ch of beg ch-4.

Rnd 2: Ch 3, dc in each st around, join in top of beg ch-3.

Rnds 3–6: [Rep rnds 1 and 2] twice.

Rnd 7: Rep rnd 2. Fasten off. ●

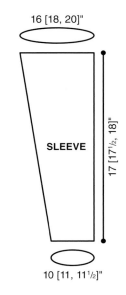

16 [18, 20]"

SLEEVE

17 [17½, 18]"

10 [11, 11½]"

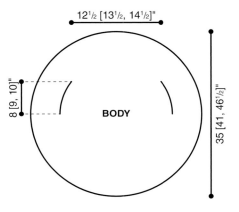

12½ [13½, 14½]"

8 [9, 10]"

BODY

35 [41, 46½]"

Seven Seas Wrap

Design by Jill Hanratty

SKILL LEVEL
Easy

FINISHED SIZES
Instructions given fit size small/medium; changes for large/X-large are in [ ].

FINISHED MEASUREMENTS
Width: 51¾ [56] inches

Length From Shoulder: 28¼ inches

MATERIALS
- Berroco Vintage medium (worsted) weight acrylic/wool/nylon yarn (3½ oz/218 yds/100g per skein):

  8 [9] skeins #5106 smoke
- Size K/10½/6.5mm crochet hook or size needed to obtain gauge
- Tapestry needle

GAUGE
20 sts and 8 rows = 4 inches in pattern; 20 sts and 10 rows = 4 inches for pockets

Take time to check gauge.

PATTERN NOTE
Join with slip stitch as indicated unless otherwise stated.

SPECIAL STITCH
V-stitch (V-st): (Tr, ch 1, tr) in st or sp indicated.

PATTERN STITCH
Pattern row: Ch 1, sk first sc, *(sc, ch 2, sc) in next ch-2 sp**, sk next 2 sc, rep from * across, ending last rep at **, turn leaving last sc unworked.

WRAP

BACK
Row 1 (WS): Ch 260 [281], sc in 2nd ch from hook, *ch 2, sk next ch**, sc in next 2 chs, rep from * across, ending last rep at **, sc in last ch, turn. (174 [188] sc, 86 [93] ch-2 sps)

Rows 2–57: [Work **pattern row** (see Pattern Stitch)] 56 times, fasten off.

Right Armhole
Row 1: On RS of Right Back at side edge, sk first 20 rows from hem, join yarn in next row, ch 1, (sc, ch 2, sc) in same row, [sk next row, (sc, ch 2, sc) in next row 36 times, turn leaving rem rows unworked. (74 sc, 37 ch-2 sps)

Row 2: [Work pattern row], fasten off.

Left Armhole
Row 1: On WS of Left Back at side edge, sk first 20 rows from hem, join yarn in next row, ch 1, (sc, ch 2, sc) in same row, [sk next row, (sc, ch 2, sc) in next row] 36 times, turn leaving rem rows unworked. (74 sc, 37 ch-2 sps)

Row 2: [Work pattern row], fasten off.

RIGHT FRONT
Row 1: Working along opposite edge of beg ch, **join** (see Pattern Note) yarn on RS in first ch-1 sp, ch 1, (sc, ch 2, sc) in same sp, [sk next 2 chs, (sc, ch 2, sc) in next ch-1 sp] 35 [38] times, turn leaving rem sts unworked. (72 [78] sc, 36 [39] ch-2 sps)

Rows 2–57: [Work pattern row] 56 times, fasten off.

Right Armhole
Row 1: On WS of Right Front at side edge, sk first 20 rows from hem, join yarn in next row, ch 1, (sc, ch 2, sc) in same row, [sk next row, (sc, ch 2, sc) in next row] 36 times, turn leaving rem rows unworked. (74 sc, 37 ch-2 sps)

Row 2: Work pattern row, fasten off.

LEFT FRONT
Row 1: On RS, sk 43 [46] beg chs from Right Front, join yarn in next ch-1 sp, ch 1, (sc, ch 2, sc) in same sp, *sk next 2 chs, (sc, ch 2, sc) in next ch-1 sp, rep from * across, turn leaving last ch unworked. (72 [78] sc, 36 [39] ch-2 sps)

Rows 2–57: [Work pattern row] 56 times, fasten off.

Left Armhole
Row 1: On RS of Left Front at side edge, sk first 20 rows from hem, join yarn in next row, ch 1, (sc, ch 2, sc) in same row, [sk next row, (sc, ch 2, sc) in next row] 36 times, turn leaving rem rows unworked. (74 sc, 37 ch-2 sps)

Row 2: Work pattern row, fasten off.

POCKET
Make 2.

Row 1 (RS): Ch 28, sc in 2nd ch from hook and each ch across, turn. (27 sc)

Row 2: Ch 1, sc in first sc, *ch 2, sk next sc**, sc in next 2 sc, rep from * across, ending last rep at **, sc in last sc, turn. (18 sc, 9 ch-2 sps)

Row 3: Ch 1, sk first sc, *(sc, ch 2, sc) in next ch-2 sp**, sk next 2 sc, **V-st** (see Special Stitch) in next sc 2 rows below, sk next 2 sc, rep from * across, ending last rep at **, turn leaving last sc unworked. *(10 sc, 4 V-sts, 5 ch-2 sps)*

Row 4: Ch 1, sk first sc, *(sc, ch 2, sc) in next ch-2 sp**, sk next sc and next tr, (sc, ch 2, sc) in next ch-1 sp, sk next tr and next sc, rep from * across, ending last rep at **, turn leaving last sc unworked.

Row 5: Ch 1, sk first sc, *(sc, ch 2, sc) in next ch-2 sp**, sk next 2 sc, V-st in next ch-2 sp 3 rows below, sk next 2 sc, rep from * across, ending last rep at **, turn leaving last sc unworked.

Rows 6–19: [Rep rows 4 and 5, alternately] 7 times.

Row 20: Ch 1, sk first sc, *(sc, ch 2, sc) in next ch-2 sp**, sk next sc and next tr, (sc, ch 2, sc) in next ch-1 sp and ch-2 sp 3 rows below tog, sk next tr and next sc, rep from * across, ending last rep at **, fasten off, leaving last sc unworked.

FINISHING
Front & Neck Edging

Row 1: Join yarn on WS in last row of Left Front at front opening, ch 1, (sc, ch 2, sc) in same row, *[sk next row, (sc, ch 2, sc) in next row]* 28 times, sk next row and next 2 foundation chs, [(sc, ch 2, sc) in next ch-1 sp, sk next 2 chs] 14 [15] times, [rep from * to *] 28 times, turn. *(142 [144] sc, 71 [72] ch-2 sps)*

Rows 2–4: [Work pattern row] 3 times, fasten off.

Sew sides, top and bottom of armhole openings.

With last row of Pocket as top and first row as bottom, sew Pockets to Front sections approximately 4 inches in from front edge and 2 inches up from bottom edge.

Weave in ends. ●

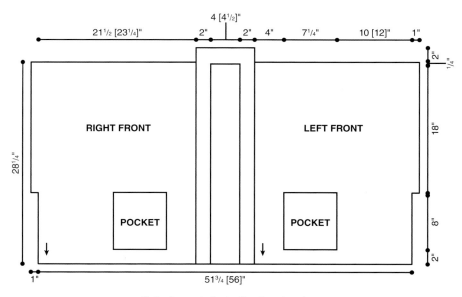

Note: *Arrows indicate direction of work.*

Moonglade Poncho

Design by Jill Hanratty

SKILL LEVEL
Intermediate

FINISHED SIZES
Instructions given fit a size small/medium; changes for large, X-large and 2X-large/3X-large are in [ ].

FINISHED MEASUREMENT
Bust: 38 *(small/medium)* [42 *(large)*, 49 *(X-large)*, 50 *(2X-large/3X-large)*] inches

MATERIALS
- Universal Yarn Uptown Worsted medium (worsted) weight acrylic yarn (3½ oz/180 yds/100g per skein): 8 [9, 10, 11] skeins #323 steel grey

  4 MEDIUM
- Size J/10/6mm crochet hook or size needed to obtain gauge
- Tapestry needle
- Stitch markers

GAUGE
Yoke and Collar: 12 sts = 4 inches; 14 rows = 4 inches

Body and Cuffs: 12 sts = 4 inches; 10 rows = 4 inches

PATTERN NOTES
"Panel" refers to each cabled section.

Weave in loose ends as work progresses.

Join with slip stitch as indicated unless otherwise stated.

Chain-3 at beginning of row counts as first double crochet.

SPECIAL STITCH
Front post treble crochet decrease (fptr dec): {Yo twice, insert hook from front to back and to front again around post of indicated st, yo, pull up lp, [yo, draw through 2 lps] twice} 4 times, yo, draw through all lps on hook.

PONCHO
YOKE
Rnd 1: Ch 58 [62, 66, 70], place marker in 3rd ch from hook, dc in 4th ch from hook *(beg sk chs count as first dc)* and each ch across, **join** *(see Pattern Notes)* in top of beg ch, turn. Using beg tail, join first and last ch. Place marker in last ch for back of Poncho and beg st of Collar. *(56 [60, 64, 68] dc)*

Rnd 2 and all even-numbered rnds: Ch 1, sc in each st around, join in first sc, turn.

Rnd 3: Ch 1, sc in first sc, sk next sc, *2 **fpdc** *(see Stitch Guide)* around next dc 2 rows below, sc in next sc, sk next dc 2 rows below and next sc, fpdc around next dc 2 rows below**, sc in next sc, sk next dc 2 rows below and next sc, rep from * around, ending last rep at **, join in first sc, turn. *(28 [30, 32, 34] sc, 42 [45, 48, 51] dc)*

Rnd 5: Ch 1, sc in first sc, *sk next sc, [fpdc around next dc 2 rows below, sc in next sc] 2 times, sk next sc, fpdc around next dc 2 rows below**, sc in next sc, rep from * around, ending last rep at **, join in first sc, turn. *(42 [45, 48, 51] sc, 42 [45, 48, 51] dc)*

Sizes Small/Medium, Large & X-Large Only
Rnd 7: Ch 1, sc in first sc, *[sk next sc, fpdc around next dc 2 rows below, sc in next sc] 6 [14, 3] times, sk next sc, 2 fpdc around next dc 2 rows below**, sc in next sc, rep from * around, ending last rep at **, join in first sc, turn. *(42 [45, 48] sc, 48 [48, 60] dc)*

Rnd 9: Ch 1, sc in first sc, *[sk next sc, fpdc around next dc 2 rows below, sc in next sc] 7 [15, 4] times, fpdc around next dc 2 rows below**, sc in next sc, rep from * around, ending last rep at **, join in first sc, turn. *(48 [48, 60] sc, 48 [48, 60] dc)*

Size 2X-Large/3X-Large Only
Rnd [7]: Ch 1, sc in first sc, ◊sk next sc, fpdc around next dc 2 rows below, sc in next sc◊, *sk next sc, 2 fpdc around next dc 2 rows below, sc in next sc**, [rep from ◊ to ◊] 5 times, rep from * around, ending last rep at **, sk next sc, fpdc around next dc 2 rows below, join in first sc, turn. *([51] sc, [60] dc)*

Rnd [9]: Ch 1, sc in first sc, *◊sk next sc, fpdc around next dc 2 rows below, sc in next sc◊, fpdc around next dc 2 rows below**, sc in next sc, [rep from ◊ to ◊] 6 times, rep from * around, ending last rep at **, sk next sc, fpdc around next dc 2 rows below, join in first sc, turn. *([60] sc, [60] dc)*

All Sizes
Rnd 11: Ch 1, sc in first sc, *sk next sc, fpdc around next dc 2 rows below**, sc in next sc, rep from * around, ending last rep at **, join in first sc, turn.

Rnd 12: Rep rnd 2.

BODY
Rnd 1: Ch 1, [sl st in next sc] 1 [1, 2, 2] time(s), **ch 3** *(see Pattern Notes)*, fptr around first dc [dc, sc, sc] 2 rows below, *ch 1, sk next sc, dc in next sc, sk next 2 dc 2 rows below, 2 **fpdtr** *(see Stitch Guide)* around next dc 2 rows below, sk next 1 [1, 2, 2] sc, dc in next sc, 2 fpdtr around first sk dc 2 rows below, sk next 1 [1, 2, 2] sc, dc in next sc, ch 1, sk next sc**, dc in next sc, fptr around next dc [dc, sc, sc] 2 rows below, rep from * around, ending last rep at **, join in top of beg ch-3, turn. *(132 sts)*

Rnd 2 and all even-numbered rnds: Ch 1, sc in 3rd ch of beg ch-3, *ch 1, sk next ch-1**, sc in each st around to next ch-1, rep from * around, ending last rep at **, sc in last st, join in first sc, turn.

Rnd 3: Ch 3, fptr around beg ch-3 2 rows below, *ch 1, sk next sc and ch-1, dc in next 2 sc, ◊fptr around next 2 dtr 2 rows below, sk next sc◊, dc in next sc, rep from ◊ to ◊, dc in next 2 sc, ch 1, sk next ch-1**, dc in next sc, fptr around next dc 2 rows below, rep from * around, ending last rep at **, join in top of beg ch-3, turn. *(156 sts)*

Rnd 5: Ch 3, fptr around beg ch-3 2 rows below, *ch 1, sk next sc and ch-1, dc in next 2 [3, 3, 3] sc, ◊fptr around next 2 tr 2 rows below, sk next 2 [1, 1, 1] sc◊, dc in next sc, rep from ◊ to ◊, dc in next 2 [3, 3, 3] sc, ch 1, sk next ch-1**, dc in next sc, fptr around next dc 2 rows below, rep from * around, ending last rep at **, join in top of beg ch-3, turn. *(156 [180, 180, 180] sts)*

Rnd 7: Ch 3, fptr around beg ch-3 2 rows below, *ch 1, sk next sc and ch-1, dc in next 2 [3, 4, 4] sc, sk next 2 tr 2 rows below, fpdtr around next 2 tr 2 rows below, sk next 2 [2, 1, 1] sc, dc in next sc, fpdtr around 2 sk tr 2 rows below, sk next 2 [2, 1, 1] sc, dc in next 2 [3, 4, 4] sc, ch 1, sk next ch-1**, dc in next sc, fptr around next dc 2 rows below, rep from * around, ending last rep at **, join in top of beg ch-3, turn.

Rnd 9: Ch 3, fptr around beg ch-3 2 rows below, *ch 1, sk next sc and ch-1, dc in next 3 [4, 5, 5] sc, ◊fptr around next 2 dtr 2 rows below, sk next sc◊, dc in next sc, rep from ◊ to ◊, dc in next 3 [4, 5, 5] sc, ch 1, sk next ch-1**, dc in next sc, fptr around next dc 2 rows below, rep from * around, ending last rep at **, join in top of beg ch-3, turn. *(180 [204, 228, 228] sts)*

Rnd 11: Ch 3, fptr around beg ch-3 2 rows below, *ch 1, sk next sc and ch-1, dc in next 1 [2, 3, 4] sc, fpdtr around next 2 tr 2 rows below, sk next 2 [2, 2, 1] sc, dc in next sc, 2 fpdtr around last dc before same 2 tr 2 rows below, sk next sc, dc in next sc, sk next 2 tr 2 rows below, 2 fpdtr around next dc 2 rows below, sk next sc, dc in next sc, fpdtr around 2 sk tr 2 rows below, sk next 2 [2, 2, 1] sc, dc in next 1 [2, 3, 4] sc, ch 1, sk next ch-1**, dc in next sc, fptr around next dc 2 rows below, rep from * around, ending last rep at **, join in top of beg ch-3, turn. *(204 [228, 252, 276] sts)*

Rnd 13: Ch 3, fptr around beg ch-3 2 rows below, *ch 1, sk next sc and ch-1, dc in next 1 [2, 3, 4] sc *(beg of each Panel)*, ◊fptr around next 2 dtr 2 rows below, sk next sc◊, dc in next sc, sk next 2 dtr 2 rows below, fpdtr around next 2 dtr 2 rows below, sk next 2 sc, dc in next sc, fpdtr around 2 sk dtr 2 rows below, sk next 2 sc, dc in next sc, rep from ◊ to ◊, dc in next 1 [2, 3, 4] sc *(end of each Panel)*, ch 1, sk next ch-1**, dc in next sc, fptr around next dc 2 rows below, rep from * around, ending last rep at **, join in top of beg ch-3, turn.

Rnd 15: Ch 3, fptr around beg ch-3 2 rows below, *ch 1, sk next sc and ch-1, dc in next 1 [2, 3, 4] sc *(beg of each Panel)*, ◊fptr around next 2 tr 2 rows below, sk next 2 sc◊, [dc in next sc, fptr around next 2 dtr 2 rows below, sk next 2 sc] 2 times, dc in next sc, rep from ◊ to ◊, dc in next 1 [2, 3, 4] sc *(end of each Panel)*, ch 1, sk next ch-1**, dc

in next sc, fptr around next dc 2 rows below, rep from * around, ending last rep at **, join in top of beg ch-3, turn.

Rnd 17: Ch 3, fptr around beg ch-3 2 rows below, *ch 1, sk next sc and ch-1, dc in next 1 [2, 3, 4] sc *(beg of each Panel)*, ◊sk next 2 tr 2 rows below, fpdtr around next 2 tr 2 rows below, sk next 2 sc, dc in next sc, fpdtr around 2 sk tr 2 rows below, sk next 2 sc◊, dc in next sc, rep from ◊ to ◊, dc in next 1 [2, 3, 4] sc *(end of each Panel)*, ch 1, sk next ch-1**, dc in next sc, fptr around next dc 2 rows below, rep from * around, ending last rep at **, join in top of beg ch-3, turn.

Rnd 19: Work rnd 13 with 2 [3, 4, 5] dc at beg and end of each Panel. *(228 [252, 276, 300] sts)*

Rnd 21: Work rnd 15 with 2 [3, 4, 5] dc at beg and end of each Panel.

Rnd 23: Work rnd 17 with 2 [3, 4, 5] dc at beg and end of each Panel.

Rnd 25: Ch 3, fptr around beg ch-3 2 rows below, *ch 1, sk next sc and ch-1, dc in next 2 [3, 4, 5] sc, ◊fptr around next 2 dtr 2 rows below, sk next 2 sc◊, dc in next sc, sk next 2 dtr 2 rows below, fpdtr around next 2 dtr 2 rows below, sk next 2 sc, dc in next sc, fpdtr around 2 sk dtr 2 rows below, sk next 2 sc, dc in next sc, rep from ◊ to ◊, dc in next 2 [3, 4, 5] sc, ch 1, sk next ch-1**, dc in next sc, fptr around next dc 2 rows below, rep from * around, ending last rep at **, join in top of beg ch-3, turn.

Rnds 26–30: Rep rnds 20–24 consecutively.

Rnd 31: Work rnd 13 with 3 [4, 5, 6] dc at beg and end of each Panel. *(252 [276, 300, 324] sts)*

Rnd 33: Work rnd 15 with 3 [4, 5, 6] dc at beg and end of each Panel.

Rnd 35: Work rnd 17 with 3 [4, 5, 6] dc at beg and end of each Panel.

Rnd 37: Work rnd 25 with 3 [4, 5, 6] dc at beg and end of each Panel.

Rnds 38–42: Rep rnds 32–36 consecutively.

Rnd 43: Work rnd 13 with 4 [5, 6, 7] dc at beg and end of each Panel. *(276 [300, 324, 348] sts)*

Rnd 45: Ch 3, fptr around beg ch-3 2 rows below, *ch 1, sk next sc and ch-1, dc in next 4 [5, 6, 7] sc, ◊fptr around next 2 tr 2 rows below, sk next 2 sc◊, [dc in next sc, fpdtr around next 2 dtr 2 rows below, sk next 2 sc] 2 times, dc in next sc, rep from ◊ to ◊, dc in next 4 [5, 6, 7] sc, ch 1, sk next ch-1**, dc in next sc, fptr around next dc 2 rows below, rep from * around, ending last rep at **, join in top of beg ch-3, turn.

Rnd 47: Ch 3, fptr around beg ch-3 2 rows below, *ch 1, sk next sc and ch-1, dc in next 4 [5, 6, 7] sc, sk next 2 tr 2 rows below, fpdtr around next 2 tr 2 rows below, sk next 2 sc, dc in next sc, fpdtr around 2 sk tr 2 rows below, sk next 2 sc, dc in next sc, sk next 2 tr 2 rows below, fpdtr around next 2 tr 2 rows below, sk next 2 sc, dc in next sc, working behind last 2 fpdtr, fptr in 2 sk tr 2 rows below, sk next 2 sc, dc in next 4 [5, 6, 7] sc, ch 1, sk next ch-1**, dc in next sc, fptr around next dc 2 rows below, rep from * around, ending last rep at **, join in top of beg ch-3, turn.

Rnd 49: Ch 3, fptr around beg ch-3 2 rows below, *ch 1, sk next sc and ch-1, dc in next 9 [11, 13, 15] sc, **fptr dec** *(see Special Stitch)* around next 4 dtr 2 rows below, sk next sc, dc in next 9 [11, 13, 15] sc, ch 1, sk next ch-1**, dc in next sc, fptr around next dc 2 rows below, rep from * around, ending last rep at **, join in top of beg ch-3, turn.

Bottom Band

Rnd 1: Ch 1, sl st in first ch-1 sp and next dc, ch 1, sc in same dc, *[sc in each st to next ch-1, ch 1, sk next ch-1]

8 times*, sc in next 19 [21, 23, 25] sts, sk next 28 [30, 34, 36] sts, rep from * to *, sc in next 18 [20, 20, 22] sts, sk next 28 [30, 34, 36] sts, join in first sc, turn *(Cuff Openings made)*. *(220 [240, 256, 276] sts)*

Rnd 2: Ch 3, *dc in each sc** to next ch-1, ch 1, sk next ch-1, dc in next sc, fptr around dc 2 rows below, ch 1, sk next ch-1, rep from * around, ending last rep at **, join in top of beg ch-3, **do not turn**.

Rnd 3: Ch 1, **reverse sc** *(see Stitch Guide)* in each st and ch-1 sp around, join in first sc, fasten off.

Cuff

Work twice.

Rnd 1: On RS, join yarn in first st at bottom of Cuff Opening, ch 3, dc in each st and ch-1 sp around, join, do not turn. *(28, [30, 34, 36] dc)*

Rnd 2: Ch 3, *fpdc around next dc**, **bpdc** *(see Stitch Guide)* around next dc, rep from * around, ending last rep at **, join in top of beg ch-3, do not turn.

Rnds 3–12: [Rep rnd 2] 10 times, fasten off.

Collar

Rnd 1: Join yarn on RS in marked ch, working in opposite edge of foundation ch, ch 1, sc in each ch around, join in first sc, turn. *(56 [60, 64, 68] sc)*

Rnd 2: Ch 1, sc in first sc, *fpdc around next dc 2 rows below**, sc in next sc, rep from * around, ending last rep at **, join in first sc, turn.

Rnd 3 and all odd-numbered rnds: Ch 1, sc in each st around, join in first sc, turn.

Rnds 4–7 [4–7, 4–9, 4–9]: [Rep rnds 2 and 3 alternately] 2 [2, 3, 3] times.

Rnd 8 [8, 10, 10]: Ch 1, sc in first sc, *sk next sc, fpdc around next dc 2 rows below, sc in next st, sk next

sc, 2 fpdc around next dc 2 rows below**, sc in next sc, rep from * around, ending last rep at **, join in first sc, turn. *(28 [30, 32, 34] sc, 42 [45, 48, 51] dc)*

Rnd 10 [10, 12, 12]: Ch 1, sc in first sc, *[sk next sc, fpdc around next dc 2 rows below, sc in next sc] 2 times, fpdc around next dc 2 rows below**, sc in next sc, rep from * around, ending last rep at **, join, turn. *(42 [45, 48, 51] sc, 42 [45, 48, 51] dc)*

Rnds 11–22 [11–22, 13–24, 13–24]: [Rep rnds 2 and 3 alternately] 6 times.

Rnd 23 [23, 25, 25]: Ch 1, reverse sc in each dc around, join, fasten off.

Finishing

Use beg tail of Cuff rnd 1 to sew gap closed at bottom of rnd. ●

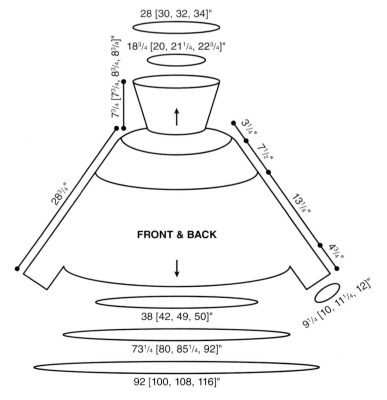

28 [30, 32, 34]"

18³/₄ [20, 21¹/₄, 22³/₄]"

7³/₄ [7³/₄, 8³/₄, 8³/₄]"

3¹/₄"

7¹/₂"

28³/₄"

13¹/₄"

4³/₄"

FRONT & BACK

38 [42, 49, 50]"

9¹/₄ [10, 11¹/₄, 12]"

73¹/₄ [80, 85¹/₄, 92]"

92 [100, 108, 116]"

Note: Arrows indicate direction of work.

Cuyama Cardi

Design by Jill Hanratty

SKILL LEVEL
Intermediate

FINISHED SIZE
Instructions given fit size small; changes for medium, large, X-large, 2X-large, 3X-large, 4X-large and 5X-large are in [ ].

FINISHED MEASUREMENTS

Bust: 38 inches *(small)* [42 inches *(medium)*; 46 inches *(large)*; 50 inches *(X-large)*; 54 inches *(2X-large)*; 58 inches *(3X-large)*; 62 inches *(4X-large)* and 66 inches *(5X-large)*]

Length: 26¼ inches *(small)* [26¼ inches *(medium)*; 26¼ inches *(large)*; 26¼ inches *(X-large)*; 27½ inches *(2X-large)*; 27½ inches *(3X-large)*; 27½ inches *(4X-large)* and 27½ inches *(5X-large)*]

MATERIALS
- Plymouth Yarn Cleo light (DK) weight cotton yarn (1¾ oz/ 125 yds/50g per hank): 8 [9, 10, 11, 12, 13, 14, 15] hanks #110 solar

  3 LIGHT
- Size H/8/5mm crochet hook or size needed to obtain gauge
- Tapestry needle
- Stitch marker

GAUGE
In Rib Pattern: 16 sts = 4 inches; 8 rows = 4 inches

In Cl Pattern: 5 clusters = 5 inches; 8 rows = 5 inches

Take time to check gauge.

PATTERN NOTES
Weave in loose ends as work progresses.

Chain-3 at beginning of row counts as first double crochet.

Treble crochet clusters count as one half-cluster for purposes of stitch counts.

Chain-4, double crochet at beginning of row counts as first treble crochet cluster.

Treble crochet in last single crochet counts as end treble crochet cluster; draw through all loops on hook in last step.

Join with slip stitch unless otherwise indicated.

SPECIAL STITCHES
Beginning cluster (beg cl): Yo, insert hook in st indicated, yo, draw up lp, yo, draw through 2 lps, keep 2 lps on hook.

End cluster (end cl): Yo, insert hook in st indicated, yo, draw up lp, yo, draw through 2 lps, yo, draw through all lps on hook.

First foundation double crochet (first foundation dc): Ch 4, yo, insert hook into 4th ch from hook, yo, pull up lp, yo, pull through 1 lp on hook *(see B in illustration)*, [yo, pull through 2 lps on hook] twice *(see D and E in illustration)*.

Next foundation double crochet (next foundation dc): [Yo, insert hook in last ch-1 made, yo, pull up lp, yo, pull through 1 lp on hook (ch-1), {yo, pull through 2 lps on hook} twice] *(see A–E in illustration)*.

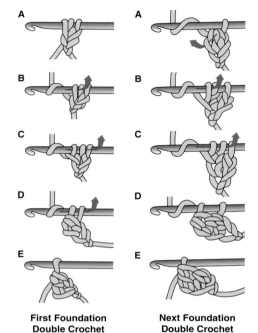

First Foundation Double Crochet

Next Foundation Double Crochet

Beginning treble cluster (beg tr cl): [Yo] twice, insert hook in st indicated, yo, draw up lp, [yo, draw through 2 lps] twice, keep 2 lps on hook.

Decrease (dec): [Yo, insert hook in st or sp indicated, yo, draw up lp, yo, draw through 2 lps] 3 times, yo, draw through all lps.

Front post decrease (fpdec): *Yo, insert hook from front to back around post of st indicated, yo, draw up lp, yo, draw through 2 lps, yo*, insert hook in next st, yo, draw up lp, yo, draw through 2 lps, rep from * to *, draw through all lps.

PATTERN STITCHES
Rib Pattern

Row 1: Ch 3 *(see Pattern Notes)*, sk first dc, ***bpdc** (see Stitch Guide)* around next dc, dc in next dc, rep from * across, turn.

Row 2 (RS): Ch 3, sk first dc, ***fpdc** (see Stitch Guide) around next dc, dc in next dc, rep from * across, turn.

Cluster Pattern (Cl Pattern)

Row 1: Ch 1, (sc, ch 2, beg cl) in first st, *sk next 5 sts**, (end cl, ch 2, sc, ch 2, beg cl) in next dc, rep from * across, ending last rep at **, (end cl, ch 2, sc) in last st, turn.

Row 2: Ch 4 (see Pattern Notes), sk first 3 sts, (dc, ch 2, sc, ch 2, beg cl) in next st, *sk next 5 sts, (end cl, ch 2, sc, ch 2, beg cl) in next st, rep from * across, sk next 2 sts, **tr in last sc** (see Pattern Notes), turn.

CARDI

RIGHT FRONT

Rib Border

Row 1 (WS): **First foundation dc** (see Special Stitches), [**next foundation dc** (see Special Stitches)] 27 [31, 35, 39, 43, 47, 51, 55] times, turn. (29 [33, 37, 41, 45, 49, 53, 57] dc)

Rows 2–5: [Work **Rib Pattern Rows 1 and 2** (see Pattern Stitches), alternately] twice, turn.

Body

Row 1: Ch 1, (sc, ch 2, **beg cl**—see Special Stitches) in first dc, *sk next 3 dc**, (**end cl**—see Special Stitches, ch 2, sc, ch 2, beg cl) in next dc, rep from * across, ending last rep at **, (end cl, ch 2, sc) in 3rd ch of beg ch-3, turn. (7 [8, 9, 10, 11, 12, 13, 14] cl)

Rows 2–30 [2–28, 2–28, 2–26, 2–28, 2–26, 2–26, 2–24]: Work **Cl Pattern Row 2** (see Pattern Stitches), then [Work **Cl Pattern Rows 1 and 2** (see Pattern Stitches), alternately] 14 [13, 13, 12, 13, 12, 12, 11] times, turn. (6 [7, 8, 9, 10, 11, 12, 13] cl, 2 half-cl)

Right Neck & Shoulder

Row 1 (RS): Ch 3, sk first 6 sts, (dc, ch 2, sc, ch 2, beg cl) in next dc, *sk next 5 sts**, (end cl, ch 2, sc, ch 2, beg cl) in next dc, rep from * across, ending last rep at **, (end cl, ch 2, sc) in last st, turn.

Row 2: Ch 4, sk first 3 sts, dc in next dc, ch 2, (sc, ch 2, beg cl) in next dc, *sk next 5 sts, (end cl, ch 2, sc, ch 2, beg cl) in next dc, rep from * across, end cl in last dc, turn. (6 [7, 8, 9, 10, 11, 12, 13] cl, 1 half-cl)

Rows 3 & 4 [3–6, 3–6, 3–6, 3–8, 3–8, 3–8, 3–8]: [Rep rows 1 and 2, alternately] 1 [2, 2, 2, 3, 3, 3, 3] time(s), turn. (5 [5, 6, 7, 7, 8, 9, 10] cl, 1 half-cl)

Rows 5–11 [7–13, 7–13, 7–15, 9–15, 9–17, 9–17, 9–19]: [Work Cl Pattern Rows 1 and 2, alternately] 3 [3, 3, 4, 3, 4, 4, 5] times, then work Cl Pattern Row 1. Do not fasten off, place marker in lp on hook until Back. (5 [5, 6, 7, 7, 8, 9, 10] cl)

LEFT FRONT

Work as for Right Front to Neck & Shoulder shaping.

Left Neck & Shoulder

Row 1: Ch 1, (sc, ch 2, beg cl) in first st, *sk next 5 sts**, (end cl, ch 2, sc, ch 2, beg cl) in next dc, rep from * across, ending last rep at **, end cl in last dc, turn.

Row 2: Ch 3, sk first 6 sts, (dc, ch 2, sc, ch 2, beg cl) in next dc, *sk next 5 sts, (end cl, ch 2, sc, ch 2, beg cl) in next dc, rep from * across, sk next 2 sts, tr in last sc, turn.

Rows 3 & 4 [3–6, 3–6, 3–6, 3–8, 3–8, 3–8, 3–8]: [Rep rows 1 and 2, alternately] 1 [2, 2, 2, 3, 3, 3, 3] time(s), turn. (5 [5, 6, 7, 7, 8, 9, 10] cl, 1 half-cl)

Rows 5–11 [7–13, 7–13, 7–15, 9–15, 9–17, 9–17, 9–19]: [Work Cl Pattern Rows 1 and 2, alternately] 3 [3, 3, 4, 3, 4, 4, 5] times, then work Cl Pattern Row 1. Fasten off. (5 [5, 6, 7, 7, 8, 9, 10] cl)

BACK

Row 1: Return lp on Right Front to hook, work Cl Pattern Row 2 across, ch 35 [43, 43, 43, 51, 51, 51, 51], **beg tr cl** (see Special Stitches) in first sc on RS of Left Shoulder, work Cl Pattern Row 2, turn. (8 [8, 10, 12, 12, 14, 16, 18] cl, 4 half-cl)

Row 2: Work Cl Pattern Row 1 across Left side, then center chs, then Right side, turn. (19 [21, 23, 25, 27, 29, 31, 33] cl)

Rows 3–35 [3–35, 3–35, 3–35, 3–37, 3–37, 3–37, 3–37]: Work in Cl Pattern as established.

Back Rib Border

Row 1: Sc in first st, *ch 3, sk next 5 sts, sc in next dc, rep from * across, turn. *(20 [22, 24, 26, 28, 30, 32, 34] sc, 19 [21, 23, 25, 27, 29, 31, 33] ch-3 sps)*

Row 2: Ch 3, sk first sc, dc in each ch and sc across, turn. *(77 [85, 93, 101, 109, 117, 125, 133] dc)*

Rows 3–6: [Work Rib Pattern Rows 1 and 2 alternately] twice, fasten off.

SLEEVE
Make 2.

Rib Border

Row 1 (RS): First foundation dc, [next foundation double crochet] 71 [71, 79, 79, 87, 87, 95, 95] times, turn. *(73 [73, 81, 81, 89, 89, 97, 97] dc)*

Rows 2–5: [Work Rib Pattern Rows 1 and 2, alternately] twice, turn.

Arm

Row 1: Ch 4, sk first 2 dc, (dc, ch 2, sc, ch 2, beg cl) in next dc, *sk next 3 dc, (end cl, ch 2, sc, ch 2, beg cl) in next dc, rep from * across, sk next dc, tr in last sc, turn. *(18 [18, 20, 20, 22, 22, 24, 24] cl)*

Rows 2–18 [2–18, 2–18, 2–18, 2–18, 2–18, 2–16, 2–16]: [Work Cl Pattern Rows 1 and 2, alternately] 8 [8, 8, 8, 8, 8, 7, 7] times, work Cl Pattern Row 1, turn.

Row 19 [19, 19, 19, 19, 19, 17, 17]: Holding Sleeve and Body RS tog, ch 3, sk first 25 [25, 23, 23, 23, 23, 21, 21] rows of Body, sl st in next row *(see Designer Tips)*, sk first 3 sts of Sleeve, dc in next dc, *[sl st in next row of Body] twice, sc in same dc of Sleeve, sl st in same row of Body, sl st in next row of Body**, **dc dec** *(see Stitch Guide)* in same dc and next dc of Sleeve, rep from * across Sleeve, ending last rep at **, **tr dec** *(see Stitch Guide)* in same dc and next dc of Sleeve, fasten off.

FINISHING
Sew side and underarm seams.

Front, Neck & Shoulder Rib

Row 1: Working in ends of rows on RS of Body, **join** *(see Pattern Notes)* yarn on RS in first row of Right Front, ch 3, dc in same row end, [2 dc in next row end] 4 times, [dc in next row end, 3 dc in next row end] 15 [14, 14, 13, 14, 13, 13, 12] times, [3 dc in next row end] twice, [2 dc in next row end] 2 [4, 4, 4, 6, 6, 6, 6] times, [dc in next row end, 3 dc in next row end] 3 [3, 3, 4, 3, 4, 4, 5] times, **dec** *(see Special Stitches)* over next 2 row ends, dec in same row end and next 2 chs, dec in next 3 chs, dc in next 25 [33, 33, 33, 41, 41, 41, 41] chs, dec in next 3 chs, dec in next 2 chs and next row end, dec in same row end and next row end, [3 dc in next row end, dc in next row end] 3 [3, 3, 4, 3, 4, 4, 5] times, [2 dc in next row end] 2 [4, 4, 4, 6, 6, 6, 6] times, [3 dc in next row end] twice, [3 dc in next row end, dc in next row end] 15 [14, 14, 13, 14, 13, 13, 12] times, [2 dc in next row end] 5 times, turn. *(215 [223, 223, 223, 239, 239, 239, 239] dc)*

Row 2: Work Rib Pattern Row 1, turn.

Row 3: Work Rib Pattern Row 2 for first 93 [93, 93, 93, 97, 97, 97, 97] dc, **fpdec** *(see Special Stitches)* in next 3 sts, work in established pattern for next 23 [31, 31, 31, 39, 39, 39, 39] dc, fpdec in next 3 sts, work in established pattern across, turn. *(211 [219, 219, 219, 235, 235, 235, 235] sts)*

Rows 4 & 5: Work Rib Pattern Rows 1 and 2 alternately, turn.

Body Edging
Sl st in each dc around Front and Neck edges, ch 1, rotate to work along bottom edge, *[2 sl st in next row end] 5 times**, sl st in each dc across, rep from * to **, join in first sl st. Fasten off.

Sleeve Edging
Join yarn on WS at underarm seam of Sleeve, sl st in each dc around, join, fasten off. Rep for 2nd Sleeve. ●

Tips
Slip stitches replace chains in last row of Sleeve to join Sleeve to Body. Sleeve is stretched to match design lines of Body. The nature of the stitch pattern prevents puckering at the joining and will create a curve from Body to underarm of Sleeve.

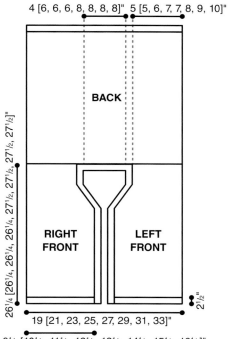

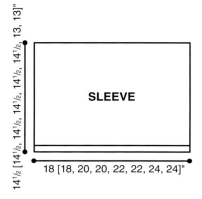

Samsara Lace Pullover

Design by Lena Skvagerson

SKILL LEVEL
Easy

FINISHED SIZES
Instructions given fit woman's size small; changes for medium, large, X-large and 2X-large are in [ ].

FINISHED MEASUREMENTS
Bust: 41 inches *(small)* [44 inches *(medium)*, 49 inches *(large)*, 53 inches *(X-large)*, 56 inches *(2X-large)*]

Length from shoulder: 23½ inches *(small)* [24 inches *(medium)*, 24½ inches *(large)*, 25 inches *(X-large)*, 25½ inches *(2X-large)*]

MATERIALS
- Cascade Yarns Sarasota light (DK) weight cotton/acrylic yarn (3½ oz/314 yds/100g per ball):
    4 [4, 4, 5, 5] balls #10 silver
- Size H/8/5mm crochet hook or size needed to obtain gauge
- Tapestry needle

GAUGE
14 dc = 4 inches; 8 dc rows = 4 inches

Take time to check gauge.

PATTERN NOTES
Front and back are worked flat separately from the top down and sewn together when finished. Sleeves are worked flat from the armhole down and sewn together when finished.

Chain-1 at beginning of rows doesn't count as a stitch.

Chain-2 at beginning of rows counts as first half double crochet unless otherwise stated.

Chain-3 at beginning of rows counts as first double crochet unless otherwise stated.

Chain-4 at beginning of rows counts as first double crochet and chain-1 unless otherwise stated.

Join with slip stitch as indicated unless otherwise stated.

SPECIAL STITCHES
Double crochet cluster (dc cl): 3 dc as indicated.

V-stitch (V-st): (Dc, ch 1, dc) as indicated.

PULLOVER
BACK
Left Shoulder
Row 1 (WS): Loosely ch 20 [22, 26, 28, 30], dc in 4th ch from hook and in each ch across, turn. *(18 [20, 24, 26, 28] dc)*

Row 2: Ch 3 *(see Pattern Notes)*, dc in each dc across, ending with dc in top of turning ch at beg of previous row, turn.

Fasten off.

Right Shoulder
Row 1 (WS): Loosely ch 20 [22, 26, 28, 30], dc in 4th ch from hook and in each ch across, turn. *(18 [20, 24, 26, 28] dc)*

Row 2: Ch 3, dc in each dc across, ending with dc in top of turning ch at beg of previous row, turn.

Back Yoke
Row 3 (WS): Ch 3, dc in each dc across right shoulder to last st, 2 dc in top of beg ch-3, loosely ch 22 [22, 22, 24, 26], 2 dc in first dc on left shoulder, dc in each dc across, ending with dc in top of turning ch at beg of previous row, turn. *(60 [64, 72, 78, 84] sts and chs)*

Row 4: Ch 2 *(see Pattern Notes)*, hdc in each dc and ch across, ending with hdc in top of turning ch at beg of previous row, turn.

Row 5: Ch 1 *(see Pattern Notes)*, sc in **back bar** *(see illustration)* of each hdc across, ending with sc in top of turning ch at beg of previous row, turn.

Half Double Crochet Back Bar (illustration shows side facing stitcher)

CH SP TEXTURE
Note: Worked on even number of sts.

Row 6: Ch 3, [dc in next sc, ch 1, sk next sc] across to last sc, dc in last sc, turn.

Rows 7–9: Ch 3, [dc in ch-1 sp, ch 1, sk next dc] across, ending with dc in top of turning ch at beg of previous row, turn.

Sizes Large, X-Large & 2X-Large Only
Rep last 2 rows once.

All Sizes
Next row (RS): Ch 2, hdc in each ch-1 sp and dc across, ending with 2 [1, 2, 2, 2] hdc in top of turning ch at beg of previous row, turn. *(61 [64, 73, 79, 85] sts)*

Next row: Rep row 5.

DC CL TEXTURE

Note: Worked in multiple of 3 sts plus 1.

Row 1 (RS): Ch 3, dc in next sc, [sk next sc, **dc cl** *(see Special Stitches)* in next sc, sk next sc] across to last 2 sc, dc in last 2 sc, turn. *(19 [20, 23, 25, 27] dc cls)*

Rows 2–4: Ch 3, dc in next dc, [sk next dc, dc cl in next dc, sk next dc] across to last 2 sts, dc in next dc, dc in top of turning ch at beg of previous row, turn.

Size 2X-Large Only

Rep last 2 rows once.

All Sizes

Next row (RS): Ch 2, hdc in each dc across, ending with hdc in top of turning ch at beg of previous row, turn.

Next row: Ch 1, sc in back bar of each hdc across, ending with sc in top of turning ch at beg of previous row, turn.

Piece measures approximately 6½ [6½, 7½, 7½, 8½] inches.

DC SECTION

Next row (RS): Ch 3, dc in each st across, turn. *(61 [64, 73, 79, 85] dc)*

Rep last row until piece *(armhole)* measures approximately 7½ [7½, 8½, 8½, 9½] inches from shoulder. Fasten off.

BACK BODY

Row 1 (RS): Loosely ch 6 [7, 7, 7, 7], dc in each dc across back yoke, loosely ch 8 [9, 9, 9, 9], turn.

Row 2: Dc in 4th ch from hook and in next 4 [5, 5, 5, 5] chs, hdc in the 61 [64, 73, 79, 85] dc across back, dc in next 6 [7, 7, 7, 7] chs, turn. *(73 [78, 87, 93, 99] sts)*

Row 3: Ch 2, hdc in each st across to last st, 1 [2, 2, 2, 2] hdc in top of turning ch at beg of previous row, turn. *(73 [79, 88, 94, 100] sts)*

Row 4: Ch 1, sc in back bar of each hdc across, ending with sc in top of turning ch at beg of previous row, turn.

V-ST TEXTURE

Note: Worked in multiple of 3 sts plus 1.

Row 1 (RS): Ch 3, dc in next sc, [sk next sc, in next sc work **V-st** *(see Special Stitches)*, sk next sc] across to last 2 sc, dc in last 2 sc, turn. *(23 [25, 28, 30, 32] V-sts)*

Rows 2–4: Ch 3, dc in next dc, [sk next dc, in next ch-1 sp work V-st, sk next dc] across to last 2 dc, dc in last 2 dc, turn.

Row 5: Ch 2, hdc in each dc and ch-1 sp across to last 2 sts;

A. sizes small and medium: sk next dc,

B. sizes large, X-large and 2X-large: work hdc in next dc,

C. All sizes: hdc in top of turning ch at beg of previous row, turn. *(72 [78, 88, 94, 100] sts)*

Row 6: Ch 1, sc in back bar of each hdc across, ending with sc in top of turning ch at beg of previous row, turn.

CH SP TEXTURE

Note: Worked on even number of sts.

Row 1 (RS): Ch 3, [dc in next sc, ch 1, sk next sc] across to last sc, dc in last sc, turn.

Rows 2–4: Ch 3, [dc in ch-1 sp, ch 1, sk next dc] across, ending with dc in top of turning ch at beg of previous row, turn.

Row 5: Ch 2, hdc in each ch-1 sp and dc across, ending with 2 [2, 1, 1, 1] hdc in last ch, turn. *(73 [79, 88, 94, 100] sts)*

Row 6: Ch 1, sc in back bar of each hdc across, ending with sc in top of turning ch at beg of previous row, turn.

RHOMB TEXTURE

Note: Worked in multiple of 3 sts plus 1.

Row 1 (RS): Ch 3, dc in next sc, [sk next sc, dc cl in next sc, sk next sc] across to last 2 sc, dc in last 2 sc, turn. *(23 [25, 28, 30, 32] dc cls)*

Row 2: Ch 3, dc in next dc, [ch 1, **dc dec** *(see Stitch Guide)* in next 3 dc, ch 1] across to last 2 sts, dc in next dc, dc in top of turning ch at beg of previous row, turn.

Row 3: Ch 3, dc in next dc, [sk next ch-1 sp, dc cl in top of next dc dec, sk next ch-1 sp] across to last 2 dc, dc in last 2 dc, turn.

Row 4: Rep row 2.

Row 5: Ch 2, hdc in each dc and in each ch across, ending with hdc in top of turning ch at beg of previous row, turn.

Row 6: Ch 1, sc in back bar of each hdc across, ending with sc in top of turning ch at beg of previous row, turn.

DC SP TEXTURE

Note: Worked in multiple of 3 sts plus 1.

Row 1 (RS): Ch 3, dc in next sc, [ch 1, sk next sc, dc in next 2 sc] across to last 2 sc, dc in last 2 sc, turn.

Rows 2–4: Ch 3, dc in next dc, [ch 1, sk next dc, dc in next 2 sts] across to last 2 sc, dc in last 2 sc, turn.

Row 5: Ch 2, hdc in each dc and ch sp across, ending with hdc in top of turning ch at beg of previous row, turn.

Row 6: Ch 1, sc in back bar of each hdc across, ending with sc in top of turning ch at beg of previous row, turn.

DC CL TEXTURE

Note: Worked in multiple of 3 sts plus 1.

Rows 1–4: Rep rows 1–4 of dc cl texture.

Row 5: Ch 2, hdc in each st across, ending with hdc in top of turning ch at beg of previous row, turn.

Row 6: Ch 1, sc in back bar of each hdc across, ending with sc in top of turning ch at beg of previous row, turn.

DC SECTION
Next row (RS): Ch 3, dc in each st across, turn.

Rep last row until piece measures approximately 16 inches from armholes.

Fasten off.

FRONT
Right Shioulder
Row 1 (WS): Loosely ch 20 [22, 26, 28, 30], dc in 4th ch from hook and in each ch across, turn. *(18 [20, 24, 26, 28] dc)*

Rows 2 & 3: Ch 3, dc in each dc across, ending with dc in top of turning ch at beg of previous row, turn.

Row 4: Ch 2, hdc in each dc across, ending with hdc in top of turning ch at beg of previous row, turn.

Row 5: Ch 1, sc in back bar of each hdc across, ending with sc in top of turning ch at beg of previous row, turn.

Row 6: Ch 3, [dc in next sc, ch 1, sk next sc] across to last sc, dc in last sc, turn.

Row 7: Ch 4 *(see Pattern Notes)*, dc in first ch-1 sp, [ch 1, sk next dc, dc in next ch-1 sp] across to last 2 sts, ch 1, sk next dc, dc in top of turning ch at beg of previous row, turn. *(19 [21, 25, 27, 29] sts)*

Row 8: Ch 3, [dc in ch-1 sp, ch 1, sk next dc] across to last ch-4 sp, in top of sp work (dc, ch 1, dc), turn. *(20 [22, 26, 28, 30] sts)*

Fasten off.

Left Shoulder
Rows 1–5: Work as rows 1–5 on right shoulder.

Row 6: Ch 3, [dc in next sc, ch 1, sk next sc] across to last sc, dc in last sc, turn.

Row 7: Ch 3, [dc in ch-1 sp, ch 1, sk next dc] across to last st, 2 dc in top of turning ch at beg of previous row, turn. *(19 [21, 25, 27, 29] sts)*

Row 8: Ch 3, dc in same st, ch 1, sk next dc, [dc in ch-1 sp, ch 1, sk next dc] across, ending with dc in top of turning ch at beg of previous row, turn. *(20 [22, 26, 28, 30] sts)*

Front Yoke
Row 9 (WS): Rep row 7 across left shoulder, do not turn, loosely ch 18 [18, 18, 20, 22], dc in first dc on right shoulder, ch 1, [dc in ch-1 sp, ch 1, sk next dc] across, ending with dc in top of turning ch at beg of previous row, turn. *(60 [64, 72, 78, 84] sts)*

Sizes Large, X-Large & 2X-Large Only
Rows 10 & 11: Ch 3, [dc in ch-1 sp, ch 1, sk next dc] across, ending with dc in top of turning ch at beg of previous row, turn.

All Sizes
Next row (RS): Ch 2, hdc in each ch-1 sp and dc across, ending with 2 [1, 2, 2, 2] hdc in top of turning ch at beg of previous row, turn. *(61 [64, 73, 79, 85] sts)*

Next row: Rep row 5.

FRONT YOKE (CONTINUED) & BODY
Starting with dc cl texture continue as on back to the final measurement.

ASSEMBLY
Sew shoulder seams.

SLEEVES
Notes: *Worked from armhole and down. Sts are worked evenly along the straight armhole edge (not over chs on each side of front and back piece).*

Row 1 (RS): Join *(see Pattern Notes)* in first st at bottom of armhole, ch 2, 55 [55, 61, 61, 67] hdc evenly along the straight armhole edge to bottom of armhole in opposite side, turn. *(56 [56, 62, 62, 68] hdc)*

Row 2: Ch 1, sc in back bar of each hdc across, ending with sc in top of turning ch at beg of previous row, turn.

Row 3: Ch 3, dc in each sc across, turn.

Row 4: Ch 3, dc in each dc across, ending with dc in top of turning ch at beg of previous row, turn.

Rows 5 & 6: Ch 3, dc dec in next 2 dc, dc in each dc across, ending with dc in top of turning ch at beg of previous row, turn. *(54 [54, 60, 60, 66] dc after row 6)*

Row 7: Ch 2, hdc in each dc across, ending with hdc in top of turning ch at beg of previous row, turn.

Row 8: Ch 1, working in back bar of each hdc across, **sc dec** *(see Stitch Guide)* in first 2 hdc, sc in each hdc across to last 3 sts, sc dec in next 2 hdc, sc in top of turning ch at beg of previous row, turn. *(52 [52, 58, 58, 64] sc)*

CH SP TEXTURE
Note: Worked on even number of sts.

Row 9: Ch 3, [dc in next sc, ch 1, sk next sc] across to last sc, dc in last sc, turn.

Rows 10–12: Ch 3, [dc in ch-1 sp, ch 1, sk next dc] across, ending with dc in top of turning ch at beg of previous row, turn.

Row 13: Ch 2, hdc in each ch-1 sp and dc across, ending with hdc in top of turning ch at beg of previous row, turn.

Row 14: Ch 1, sc in back bar of each hdc across, ending with sc in top of turning ch at beg of previous row, turn. *(52 [52, 58, 58, 64] sc)*

DC CL TEXTURE
Note: Worked in multiple of 3 sts plus 1.

Row 15 (RS): Ch 3, dc in next dc, [sk next sc, dc cl in next sc, sk next sc] across to last 2 sc, dc in last 2 sc, turn. *(16 [16, 18, 18, 20] dc cls)*

Rows 16–18: Ch 3, dc in next dc, [sk next dc, dc cl in next dc, sk next dc] across to last 2 sts, dc in next dc, dc in top of turning ch at beg of previous row, turn.

Row 19: Ch 2, hdc in each dc across to last 3 sts, **hdc dec** *(see Stitch Guide)* in next 2 sts, hdc in top of turning ch at beg of previous row, turn. *(51 [51, 57, 57, 63] hdc)*

Row 20: Rep row 8. *(49 [49, 55, 55, 61] sc)*

V-ST TEXTURE
Note: Worked in multiple of 3 sts plus 1.

Row 21 (RS): Ch 3, dc in next sc, [sk next sc, in next sc work V-st, sk next sc] across to last 2 sc, dc in last 2 sc, turn. *(15 [15, 17, 17, 19] V-sts)*

Rows 22–24: Ch 3, dc in next dc, [sk next dc, in next ch-1 sp work V-st, sk next dc] across to last 2 dc, dc in next dc, dc in top of turning ch at beg of previous row, turn.

Rows 25 & 26: Rep rows 7 and 8. *(47 [47, 53, 53, 59] sc)*

DC SECTION
Next row (RS): Ch 3, (dc in next 3 [3, 4, 4, 4] dc, dc dec in next 2 sc) across to last 6 [6, 4, 4, 4] sts, dc in each rem sc, dc in top of turning ch at beg of previous row, turn. *(39 [39, 45, 45, 50] dc)*

Next row: Ch 3, dc in each dc across, ending with dc in top of turning ch at beg of previous row, turn.

Rep last row until sleeve measures approximately 11 [11½, 11½, 11½, 11½] inches from shoulder. Fasten off.

Rep in opposite side.

ASSEMBLY
Sew upper sides of sleeves on each side to ch sts at bottom of armhole. Starting at cuff opening, sew sleeve seam up to armhole and continue with side seam from armhole and down, leaving a 2½-inch split at the bottom of side.

Rep on other side.

Neck Edge
Join yarn at shoulder seam, ch 1, sc in same st, [ch 3, sk ½ inch, sc in next st] around, ending with ch 3, sl st in first sc at beg of rnd.

Fasten off.

FINISHING
Weave in ends. ●

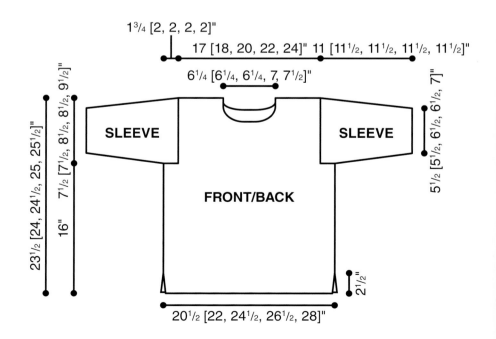

Seashell Cardi

Design by Lena Skvagerson

SKILL LEVEL
Easy

FINISHED SIZES
Instructions given fit size small; changes for medium, large, X-large, 2X-large and 3X-large are in [ ].

FINISHED MEASUREMENTS
Cardi Bust: 38 inches *(small)* [42 inches *(medium)*, 46 inches *(large)*, 50 inches *(X-large)*, 54 inches *(2X-large)*, 58 inches *(3X-large)*]

Cardi Length: 25 inches *(small)* [25½ inches *(medium)*, 26 inches *(large)*, 26½ inches *(X-large)*, 27 inches *(2X-large)*, 27½ inches *(3X-large)*]

MATERIALS
- Omega Mimosa fine (sport) weight cotton/rayon yarn (3½ oz/240 yds/100g per ball): 6 [7, 7, 8, 9, 10] balls #19 cream

  2 FINE
- Size G/6/4mm crochet hook or size needed to obtain gauge
- Locking stitch markers
- Tapestry needle

GAUGE
17 dc = 4 inches; 11 dc rows = 4 inches

Take time to check gauge.

PATTERN NOTES
Weave in ends as work progresses.

Chain-2 at beginning of row counts as first half double crochet unless otherwise stated.

Chain-3 at beginning of row counts as first double crochet unless otherwise stated.

Chain-4 at beginning of row counts as first double crochet and chain-1 unless otherwise stated.

Join with slip stitch as indicated unless otherwise stated.

SPECIAL STITCH
Shell: 6 dc in 1 st or sp as indicated in instructions.

CARDI

LOWER BODY
Row 1 (RS): With cream, loosely ch 161 [177, 193, 213, 229, 245], dc in 4th ch from hook and in each ch across, turn. *(159 [175, 191, 211, 227, 243] dc)*

Rows 2 & 3: Ch 3 *(see Pattern Notes)*, dc in each dc across, ending with dc in top of beg ch-3, turn.

Row 4 (WS): Ch 3, dc in next 2 dc, [ch 1, sk next st, dc in next 3 dc] across, turn.

Row 5: Ch 3, dc in each dc and ch sp across, ending with dc in top of beg ch-3, turn.

Rep [rows 4 and 5] until piece measures 6½ [6¼, 6½, 6¼, 6½, 6¾] inches, ending with a RS row.

Work 2 Texture Rows
Next row (WS): Ch 4 *(see Pattern Notes)*, fpdtr *(see Stitch Guide)* in each dc across, ending with tr in top of beg ch-3, turn.

Next row: Ch 2 *(see Pattern Notes)*, bpdc *(see Stitch Guide)* in each dtr across, ending with hdc in beg ch-4, turn.

Continue working [rows 4 and 5] until piece measures 14 [13½, 14, 13½, 14, 14½] inches, ending with a RS row.

Rep 2 texture rows.

Continue working [rows 4 and 5] until piece measures 17 [16½, 17, 16½, 17, 17½] inches, ending with a WS row.

Count 39 [43, 47, 52, 56, 60] sts in from each side and place a marker before next st; 81 [89, 97, 107, 115, 123] sts between markers for back piece.

RIGHT FRONT
Armhole Shaping
Row 1 (RS): Ch 3, dc in next 32 [36, 38, 41, 41, 45] sts, turn leaving last 6 [6, 8, 10, 14, 14] sts before first marker unworked. *(33 [37, 39, 42, 42, 46] dc)*

Sizes Small, Medium & Large Only
Row 2: Ch 3, **dc dec** *(see Stitch Guide)* in next 2 dc, work in established pattern across, making sure ch sps line up above each other, turn. *(32 [36, 38] sts)*

Row 3: Ch 3, dc in each dc and ch sp across to last 2 dc, dc dec in last 2 dc, turn. *(31 [35, 37] sts)*

Row 4: Ch 3, dc dec in next 2 dc, work in established pattern across, making sure ch sps line up above each other, turn. *(30 [34, 36] sts)*

Sizes Medium & Large Only
Row [5]: Ch 3, dc in each dc and ch sp across to last 2 dc, dc dec in last 2 dc, turn. *([33, 35] sts)*

Size Large Only
Row [6]: Ch 3, dc dec in next 2 dc, work in established pattern across, making sure ch sps line up above each other, turn. *([34] dc)*

Sizes X-Large, 2X-Large & 3X-Large Only
Row [2] (WS): Sl st in first 3 sts, ch 3, work in established pattern across, making sure ch sps line up above each other, turn. *([40, 40, 44] dc)*

Size X-Large Only
Row [3]: Ch 3, dc in each dc and ch sp across to last 2 dc, dc dec in last 2 dc, turn. *([39] dc)*

Row [4]: Ch 3, dc dec in next 2 dc, work in established pattern across, making sure ch sps line up above each other, turn. *([38] dc)*

Rows [5–8]: Rep [rows 3 and 4] 2 times. *([34] dc)*

Size 2X-Large Only
Row [3]: Ch 3, dc in each dc and ch sp across to last 2 dc, dc dec in last 2 dc, turn. *([39] dc)*

Row [4]: Ch 3, dc dec in next 2 dc, work in established pattern across, making sure ch sps line up above each other, turn. *([38] dc)*

Rows [5–7]: Rep rows 3 and 4, then rep row 3. *([35] dc)*

Size 3X-Large Only
Row [3]: Ch 3, dc in each dc and ch sp across to last 2 dc, turn leaving last 2 dc unworked. *([42] dc)*

Row [4]: Ch 3, [dc dec in next 2 dc] twice, work in established pattern across, making sure ch sps line up above each other, turn. *([40] dc)*

Row [5]: Ch 3, dc in each dc and ch sp across to last 2 dc, dc dec in last 2 dc, turn. *([39] dc)*

Row [6]: Ch 3, dc dec in next 2 dc, work in established pattern across, making sure ch sps line up above each other, turn. *([38] dc)*

Rows [7 & 8]: Rep [rows 5 and 6]. *([36] dc)*

All Sizes
Work even in established pattern until piece measures 4 [4½, 4½, 5, 5, 5] inches from beg of Armhole Shaping, ending with a RS row.

Neck Shaping
Row 1 (WS): Ch 3, work in established pattern across to last 6 sts, making sure ch sps line up above each other, turn, leaving rem sts unworked. *(24 [27, 28, 28, 29, 30] dc)*

Row 2: Ch 3, dc dec in next 2 dc, work dc in each dc and ch sp across, turn. *(23 [26, 27, 27, 28, 29] dc)*

Row 3: Ch 3, work in established pattern across to last 2 sts, making sure ch sps line up above each other, dc dec in last 2 sts, turn. *(22 [25, 26, 26, 27, 28] dc)*

Rows 4 & 5: Rep rows 2 and 3 once. *(20 [23, 24, 24, 25, 26] dc)*

Row 6: Ch 3, dc dec in next 2 dc, work dc in each dc across, turn. *(19 [22, 23, 23, 24, 25] sts rem on shoulder)*

Work even in established pattern until piece measures 7 [8, 8, 9, 9, 9] inches from beg of Armhole Shaping.

Fasten off.

BACK
Armhole Shaping
Row 1 (RS): With RS facing, **join** *(see Pattern Notes)* yarn in 7th [7th, 7th, 9th, 11th, 15th] st after first marker, ch 3, work in established pattern across, leaving last 6 [6, 8, 10, 14, 14] sts before next marker unworked, turn. *(69 [77, 81, 87, 87, 95] sts)*

Sizes Small, Medium & Large Only
Next 3 [4, 5] rows: Work even in established pattern, making sure ch sps line up above each other, and at the same time, work dc dec at beg and end of every row. *(63 [69, 71] sts at end of last row worked)*

Sizes X-Large, 2X-Large & 3X-Large Only
Row(s) [2, 2, 2–4]: Ch 3, [dc dec in next 2 dc] twice, work in established pattern across to last 4 sts, [dc dec in next 2 dc] twice, turn. *([83, 83, 91] sts)*

Next rows: Work in established pattern and at the same time, work dc dec at beg and end of every row [6, 5, 4] times. *([71, 73, 75] sts at end of last row)*

All Sizes
Work even in established pattern until piece measures 7 [8, 8, 9, 9, 9] inches from beg of Armhole Shaping. *(63 [69, 71, 71, 73, 75] sts)*

Fasten off.

From each outside edge, count 19 [22, 23, 23, 24, 25] sts, placing a marker in last counted st, leaving 25 sts in the center for neck opening.

LEFT FRONT
Armhole Shaping
Row 1 (RS): With RS facing, join yarn in 7th [7th, 7th, 9th, 11th, 15th] st after 2nd marker, ch 3, work in established pattern across, turn. *(33 [37, 39, 42, 42, 46] dc)*

Sizes Small, Medium & Large Only
Row 2 (WS): Ch 3, work in established pattern across to last 2 sts, making sure ch sps line up above each other, dc dec in last 2 dc, turn. *(32 [36, 38] dc)*

Row 3: Ch 3, dc dec in next 2 dc, dc in each dc and ch sp across, turn. *(31 [35, 37] dc)*

Row 4: Ch 3, work in established pattern across to last 2 sts, making sure ch sps line up above each other, dc dec in last 2 dc, turn. *(30 [34, 36] dc)*

Sizes Medium & Large Only
Row [5]: Ch 3, dc dec in next 2 dc, dc in each dc and ch sp across, turn. *([33, 35] dc)*

Size Large Only
Row [6]: Ch 3, work in established pattern across to last 2 sts, making sure ch sps line up above each other, dc dec in last 2 dc, turn. *([34] dc)*

Sizes X-Large, 2X-Large & 3X-Large Only
Row [2] (WS): Ch 3, work in established pattern across to last 4 sts, making sure ch sps line up above each other, [dc dec in next 2 sts] twice, turn. *([40, 40, 44] dc)*

Size X-Large Only
Row [3]: Ch 3, dc dec in next 2 dc, dc in each dc and ch sp across, turn. *([39] dc)*

Row [4]: Ch 3, work in established pattern across to last 2 sts, making sure ch sps line up above each other, dc dec in last 2 dc, turn. *([38] dc)*

Rows [5–8]: Rep [rows 3 and 4] 2 times. ([34] dc)

Size 2X-Large Only

Row [3]: Ch 3, dc dec in next 2 dc, dc in each dc and ch sp across, turn. ([39] dc)

Row [4]: Ch 3, work in established pattern across to last 2 sts, making sure ch sps line up above each other, dc dec in last 2 dc, turn. ([38] dc)

Rows [5–7]: Rep rows 3 and 4, then rep row 3. ([35] dc)

Size 3X-Large Only

Row [3]: Ch 3, [dc dec in next 2 dc] twice, dc in each dc and ch sp across, turn. ([42] dc)

Row [4]: Ch 3, work in established pattern across to last 4 sts, making sure ch sps line up above each other, [dc dec in next 2 dc] twice, turn. ([40] dc)

Row [5]: Ch 3, dc dec in next 2 dc, dc in each dc and ch sp across, turn. ([39] dc)

Row [6]: Ch 3, work in established pattern across to last 2 sts, making sure ch sps line up above each other, dc dec in last 2 dc, turn. ([38] dc)

Rows [7 & 8]: Rep [rows 5 and 6]. ([36] dc)

All Sizes

Work even in established pattern until piece measures 4 [4½, 4½, 5, 5, 5] inches from beg of Armhole Shaping, ending with a RS row. Fasten off.

Neck Shaping

Row 1 (WS): Sk first 6 sts, join yarn in 7th st, ch 3, work in established pattern across, making sure ch sps line up above each other, turn. (24 [27, 28, 28, 29, 30] dc)

Row 2: Ch 3, work dc in each dc and ch sp across to last 2 sts, dc dec in last 2 sts, turn. (23 [26, 27, 27, 28, 29] dc)

Row 3: Ch 3, dc dec in next 2 sts, work in established pattern across, making sure ch sps line up above each other, turn. (22 [25, 26, 26, 27, 28] dc)

Rows 4 & 5: Rep rows 2 and 3 once. (20 [23, 24, 24, 25, 26] dc)

Row 6: Ch 3, work dc in each dc and ch sp across to last 2 sts, dc dec in last 2 sts, turn. (19 [22, 23, 23, 24, 25] sts rem on shoulder)

Work even in established pattern until piece measures 7 [8, 8, 9, 9, 9] inches from beg of Armhole Shaping.

Fasten off.

SLEEVE

Make 2.

Row 1 (RS): Loosely ch 55 [67, 67, 73, 73, 73], dc in 4th ch from hook and in each ch across, turn. (53 [65, 65, 71, 71, 71] dc)

Rows 2 & 3: Ch 3, dc in each dc across, ending with dc in top of beg ch-3, turn.

Row 4: Ch 3, dc in next 1 [1, 1, 2, 2, 2] dc, [ch 1, sk next st, dc in next 3 dc] across to last 3 [3, 3, 4, 4, 4] sts, ch 1, sk next st, dc in last 2 [2, 2, 3, 3, 3] sts, turn.

Row 5: Ch 3, dc in each dc and ch sp across, turn.

Work 2 Texture Rows

Next row (WS): Ch 4, tr in same st as first ch, fpdtr in each dc across, ending with 2 tr in top of beg ch-3, turn. (55 [67, 67, 73, 73, 73] sts)

Next row: Ch 2, bpdc in each dtr across, ending with hdc in top of ch-4 at beg of previous row, turn.

Rep [rows 4 and 5], incorporating inc sts from Texture Rows into established pattern, making sure ch sps line up above each other, until piece measures 7 inches, ending with a RS row.

Rep Texture Rows. (57 [69, 69, 75, 75, 75] dc)

Rep [rows 4 and 5], incorporating inc sts into established pattern, making sure ch sps line up above each other, until piece measures 10 inches, ending with a WS row.

Cap Shaping

Row 1 (RS): Sl st in first 6 [6, 8, 11, 11, 11] sts, ch 3, work dc in each dc across leaving last 5 [5, 7, 10, 10, 10] sts unworked, turn. (47 [59, 55, 55, 55, 55] sts)

Sizes Small, Medium & Large Only

Next rows: Work even in established pattern, making sure ch sps line up above each other, and at the same time, work dc dec at beg and end of every row 8 [10, 10] times, then work [dc dec] twice at beg and end of next 2 [1, 3] row(s), then work [dc dec] 3 times at beg and end of next 0 [2, 0] rows, work 1 row even. (23 [23, 23] sts left)

Fasten off.

Sizes X-Large, 2X-Large & 3X-Large Only

Row [2]: Sl st in first 3 sts, work in established pattern across, making sure ch sps line up above each other, leaving last 2 sts unworked, turn. ([51, 51, 51] sts)

Next rows: Work in established pattern and at the same time, work dc dec at beg and end of every row [12, 12, 12] times, then work [dc dec] twice at beg and end of next row, work 1 row even. ([23, 23, 23] sts rem)

Fasten off.

ASSEMBLY

Block pieces to measurements on schematics.

Sew shoulder seams to markers for neck opening.

Sew sleeves into armholes.

Sew sleeve seams.

CARDIGAN EDGING

Rnd 1: With RS facing, join in first st of Back after Right shoulder seam, ch 1, evenly sp sc around entire outer edge in multiples of 6 with 3 sc in each outside corner, join in beg sc.

Rnd 2: Ch 1, sc in first st, sk next 2 sc, **shell** (see Special Stitch) in next st, sk next 2 sc, [sc in next sc, sk next 2 sc, shell in next sc, sk next 2 sc] around, join in beg sc. Fasten off.

SLEEVE EDGING

Working in starting ch on opposite side of foundation ch, rep Cardigan Edging around bottom edge of each Sleeve.

FINISHING

Weave in ends.

Wet-block and lay flat in shape to dry to make flat and even. ●

SLEEVE

5"

4½ [5½, 5½, 6, 6, 6]"

10"

1"

12½ [15¼, 15¼, 16¾, 16¾, 16¾]"

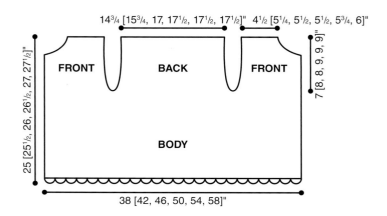

14¾ [15¾, 17, 17½, 17½, 17½]"   4½ [5¼, 5½, 5½, 5¾, 6]"

FRONT   BACK   FRONT

7 [8, 8, 9, 9, 9]"

BODY

25 [25½, 26, 26½, 27, 27½]"

38 [42, 46, 50, 54, 58]"

Paradiso Tunic

Design by Tammy Hildebrand

SKILL LEVEL
Intermediate

FINISHED SIZES
Instructions given fit size small; changes for medium, large, X-large and 2X-large are in [ ].

FINISHED MEASUREMENT
Bust: 40 [44, 48, 52, 56] inches

MATERIALS
- Patons Grace light (DK) weight mercerized cotton yarn (1¾ oz/136 yds/50g per ball):

  6 [7, 8, 9, 10] balls clay
- Size G/6/4mm crochet hook or size needed to obtain gauge
- Tapestry needle

GAUGE
2 pattern reps of 2 shells and 2 ch-5 sps = 4 inches; 8 rnds in lace pattern = 4 inches

PATTERN NOTES
Weave in loose ends as work progresses.

Join with slip stitch unless otherwise stated.

Chain-8 at beginning of round counts as first double crochet, chain-5.

Chain-3 at beginning of round counts as first double crochet.

Tunic is worked from top down with sleeves worked directly into armholes.

SPECIAL STITCHES
First foundation single crochet (first foundation sc): Ch 2, insert hook into 2nd ch from hook, yo, pull up a lp, yo, pull through 1 lp on hook *(see illustration A—ch-1 completed)*, yo, pull through both lps on hook *(see illustrations B and C—sc completed).*

Next foundation single crochet (next foundation sc): [Insert hook in last ch-1 made *(see illustration A)*, yo, pull up a lp, yo, pull through 1 lp on hook *(see illustration B—ch-1 completed)*, yo, pull through both lps on hook *(see illustrations C and D—sc completed)*] as indicated in instructions.

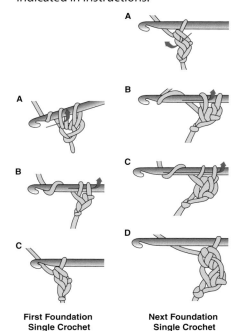

First Foundation Single Crochet

Next Foundation Single Crochet

Large V-stitch (lg V-st): (Dc, ch 5, dc) in same st.

Large shell (lg sh): 5 dc in same sp.

Shell (sh): 3 dc in same sp.

Increase (inc): [Sc, (ch 5, sc) 2 times] in same sp.

TUNIC
YOKE
Foundation row: Make **first foundation sc** *(see Special Stitches)*, make 79 [99, 119, 139, 159] **next foundation sc** *(see Special Stitches)*, turn. *(80 [100, 120, 140, 160] sts)*

Rnd 1: Ch 8 *(see Pattern Notes)*, dc in same st *(counts as first V-st)*, ch 3, sk next 4 sts, *lg V-st *(see Special Stitches)* in next st, ch 3, sk next 4 sts; rep from * around, **join** *(see Pattern Notes)* in 3rd ch of beg ch-5. *(16 [20, 24, 28, 32] lg V-sts and 16 [20, 24, 28, 32] ch-3 sps)*

Rnd 2: Sl st in next ch-5 sp, **ch 3** *(see Pattern Notes)*, 4 dc in same sp *(counts as first lg sh)*, sc in next ch-3 sp, *lg sh *(see Special Stitches)* in next ch-5 sp, sc in next ch-3 sp; rep from * around, join in top of beg ch-3. *(16 [20, 24, 28, 32] lg sh and 16 [20, 24, 28, 32] sc)*

Rnd 3: Sl st in next 2 dc, ch 1, sc in center dc of lg sh, ch 5, sc in next sc, ch 5, *sk next 2 dc, sc in next dc, ch 5, sc in next sc, ch 5; rep from * around, join in beg sc. *(32 [40, 48, 56, 64] ch-5 sps)*

Rnd 4: Sl st in next 2 chs, ch 1, **inc** *(see Special Stitches)* in same ch-5 sp, ch 5, [sc in next ch-5 sp, ch 5] 7 [9, 11, 13, 15] times, *inc in next ch-5 sp, ch 5, [sc in next ch-5 sp, ch 5] 7 [9, 11, 13, 15] times; rep from * around, join in beg sc. *(40 [48, 56, 64, 72] ch-5 sps)*

Rnd(s) 5 [5, 5 & 6, 5 & 6, 5–7]: Sl st in next 2 chs, ch 1, sc in same ch-5 sp, ch 5, *sc in next ch-5 sp, ch 5; rep from * around, join in beg sc.

Rnd 6 [6, 7, 7, 8]: Ch 3, 2 dc in same st *(counts as first sh)*, sc in next ch-5 sp, ch 5, sc in next ch-5 sp, *sh *(see Special*

Stitches) in next sc, sc in next ch-5 sp, ch 5, sc in next ch-5 sp; rep from * around, join in top of beg ch-3. *(20 [24, 28, 32, 36] sh and 20 [24, 28, 32, 36] ch-5 sps)*

Rnd 7 [7, 8, 8, 9]: Sl st in next dc, ch 1, sc in same dc, ch 5, sc in next ch-5 sp, ch 5, *sc in center dc of next sh, ch 5, sc in next ch-5 sp, ch 5; rep from * around, join in beg sc. *(40 [48, 56, 64, 72] ch-5 sps)*

Rnd 8 [8, 9, 9, 10]: Rep rnd 6 [6, 7, 7, 8].

Rnd 9 [9, 10, 10, 11]: Sl st in next dc, ch 1, sc in same center dc, ch 5, *inc in next ch-5 sp, ch 5, sc in center dc of next sh, ch 5, [sc in next ch-5 sp, ch 5, sc in center dc of next sh, ch 5] 4 [5, 6, 7, 8] times, rep from * 2 more times, inc in next ch-5 sp, ch 5, [sc in center dc of next sh, ch 5, sc in next ch-5 sp, ch 5] 4 [5, 6, 7, 8] times, join in beg sc. *(48 [56, 64, 72, 80] ch-5 sps)*

Rnd 10 [10, 11, 11, 12]: Rep rnd 6 [6, 7, 7, 8]. *(24 [28, 32, 36, 40] sh and 24 [28, 32, 36, 40] ch-5 sps)*

Rnd 11 [11, 12, 12, 13]: Sl st in next dc, ch 1, sc in same center dc, ch 5, *inc in next ch-5 sp, ch 5, sc in center dc of next sh, ch 5, [sc in next ch-5 sp, ch 5, sc in center dc of next sh, ch 5] 5 [6, 7, 8, 9] times, rep from * 2 more times, inc in next ch-5 sp, ch 5, [sc in center dc of next sh, ch 5, sc in next ch-5 sp, ch 5] 5 [6, 7, 8, 9] times, join in beg sc. *(56 [64, 72, 80, 88] ch-5 sps)*

Rnd 12 [12, 13, 13, 14]: Rep rnd 6 [6, 7, 7, 8]. *(28 [32, 36, 40, 44] sh and 28 [32, 36, 40, 44] ch-5 sps)*

Rnd 13 [13, 14, 14, 15]: Sl st in next dc, ch 1, sc in same center dc, ch 5, *inc in next ch-5 sp, ch 5, sc in center dc of next sh, ch 5, [sc in next ch-5 sp, ch 5, sc in center dc of next sh, ch 5] 6 [7, 8, 9, 10] times, rep from * 2 more times, inc in next ch-5 sp, ch 5, [sc in center dc of next sh, ch 5, sc in next ch-5 sp, ch 5] 6 [7, 8, 9, 10] times, join in beg sc. *(64 [72, 80, 88, 96] ch-5 sps)*

Rnd 14 [14, 15, 15, 16]: Rep rnd 6 [6, 7, 7, 8]. *(32 [36, 40, 44, 48] sh and 32 [36, 40, 44, 48] ch-5 sps)*

Rnd 15 [15, 16, 16, 17]: Sl st in next dc, ch 1, sc in same center dc, ch 5, *inc in next ch-5 sp, ch 5, sc in center dc of next sh, ch 5, [sc in next ch-5 sp, ch 5, sc in center dc of next sh, ch 5] 7 [8, 9, 10, 11] times, rep from * 2 more times, inc in next ch-5 sp, ch 5, [sc in center dc of next sh, ch 5, sc in next ch-5 sp, ch 5] 7 [8, 9, 10, 11] times, join in beg sc. *(72 [80, 88, 96, 104] ch-5 sps)*

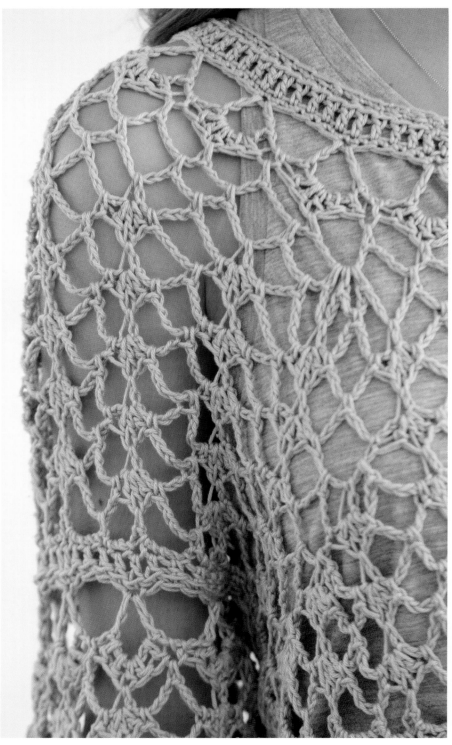

Rnd 16 [16, 17, 17, 18]: Sl st in next ch-5 sp, ch 1, 3 sc in same sp, 2 sc in next ch-5 sp, *3 sc in next ch-5 sp, 2 sc in next ch-5 sp; rep from * around, join in beg sc. *(180 [200, 220, 240, 260] sc)*

Rnd 17 [17, 18, 18, 19]: Ch 3, dc in each st around, join in top of beg ch-3.

BODY

Rnd 1: Working this rnd in **back lps** *(see Stitch Guide)* only, ch 1, sc in first st, sc in next 17 [19, 21, 23, 25] sts, hdc in next 14 [15, 16, 17, 18] sts, sc in next 18 [20, 22, 24, 26] sts, sk next 40 [45, 50, 55, 60] sts *(first armhole)*, sc in next 18 [20, 22, 24, 26] sts, hdc in next 14 [15, 16, 17, 18] sts, sc in next 18 [20, 22, 24, 26] sts, sk last 40 [45, 50, 55, 60] sts *(second armhole)*, join in beg sc. *(100 [110, 120, 130, 140] sts)*

Rnds 2–4: Rep rnds 1–3 of yoke. *(40 [44, 48, 52, 56] ch-5 sps)*

Rnds 5–12: Rep rnds 6 & 7 [6 & 7, 7 & 8, 7 & 8, 8 & 9] of yoke.

Rnd 13: Rep rnd 6 [6, 7, 7, 8] of yoke.

Rnd 14: Sl st in next dc, ch 1, sc in same center dc, ch 5, inc in next ch-5 sp, ch 5, *sc in center dc of next sh, ch 5, [sc in next ch-5 sp, ch 5, sc in center dc of next sh, ch 5] 5 times, inc in next ch-5 sp, ch 5; rep from * 2 more times [sc in center dc of next sh, ch 5, sc in next ch-5 sp, ch 5] to end, join in beg sc. *(48 [52, 56, 60, 64] ch-5 sps)*

Rnds 15 & 16: Rep rnds 16 & 17 [16 & 17, 17 & 18, 17 & 18, 18 & 19] of yoke. *(120 [130, 140, 150, 160] dc)*

Rnd 17: Ch 1, working this rnd in back lps only, sc in each st around, join in beg sc.

Rnds 18–23: Rep rnds 2–7 of body.

Rnd 24: Sl st in next dc, ch 1, sc in same center dc, ch 5, inc in next ch-5 sp, ch 5, *sc in center dc of next sh, ch 5, [sc in next ch-5 sp, ch 5, sc in center

dc of next sh, ch 5] 6 times, inc in next ch-5 sp, ch 5; rep from * 2 more times [sc in center dc of next sh, ch 5, sc in next ch-5 sp, ch 5] to end, join in beg sc. *(56 [60, 64, 68, 72] ch-5 sps)*

Rnds 25–30: Rep rnds 6 & 7 [6 & 7, 7 & 8, 7 & 8, 8 & 9] of yoke.

Rnds 31–33: Rep rnds 15–17 of body. Fasten off after last rnd.

SLEEVE

Rnd 1: With RS facing, join yarn in center of underarm, ch 1, working in back lps only, sc in each st around, sk sl st, join in first sc. *(40 [45, 50, 55, 60] sc)*

Rnds 2–4: Rep rnds 1–3 of yoke. *(16 [18, 20, 22, 24] ch-5 sps)*

Rnds 5–14: Rep rnds 6 & 7 [6 & 7, 7 & 8, 7 & 8, 8 & 9] of yoke.

Rnds 15–17: Rep rnds 15–17 of body. Fasten off after last rnd.

Rep for 2nd sleeve on opposite side.

COLLAR

Rnd 1: Working in opposite side of foundation row, join yarn in any st, ch 3, dc in next 2 sts, **dc dec** *(see Stitch Guide)* in next 2 sts, *dc in next

3 sts, dc dec in next 2 sts; rep from * around, join in top of beg ch-3. *(74 [80, 96, 112, 128] dc)*

Rnd 2: Ch 1, working this rnd in back lps only, sc in first st, sc in next 6 [2, 3, 4, 5] sts, **sc dec** *(see Stitch Guide)* in next 2 sts, *sc in next 3 sts, sc dec in next 2 sts; rep from * around, join in beg sc. *(60 [64, 77, 90, 103] sc)*

Sizes Small & Medium Only

Fasten off.

Sizes Large, X-Large & 2X-Large Only

Rnd [3]: Ch 1, sc in first st, sc in next 4 [2, 4] sts, sc dec in next 2 sts, *sc in next 5 [3, 2] sts, sc dec in next 2 sts; rep from * around, join in beg sc. Fasten off. *(66 [72, 78] sc)*

FINISHING

Weave in loose ends.

Submerge garment into cool water and gently stretch open lace pattern. Squeeze out excess water and blot dry. Spread on flat surface and pin to finished measurements. Allow to lay flat until completely dry. ●

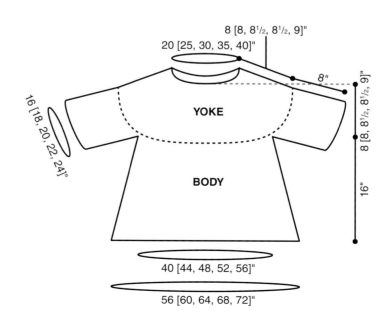

White Sand Tee

Design by Lena Skvagerson

SKILL LEVEL
Easy

FINISHED SIZES
Instructions given fit woman's size small; changes for medium, large, X-large, 2X-large and 3X-large are in [ ].

FINISHED MEASUREMENTS
Bust: 39 inches *(small)* [43 inches *(medium)*; 47 inches *(large)*; 51 inches *(X-large)*; 55 inches *(2X-large)*; 59 inches *(3X-large)*]

Length from shoulder: 21 inches *(small)* [23 inches *(medium)*; 24 inches *(large)*; 25 inches *(X-large)*; 26 inches *(2X-large)*; 27 inches *(3X-large)*]

MATERIALS
- Universal Fibra Natura Papyrus light (DK) weight cotton/ silk yarn (1¾ oz/131 yds/50g per ball):
    - 6 [7, 8, 9, 10, 11] balls #01 cloud
- Size H/8/5mm crochet hook or size needed to obtain gauge
- Tapestry needle

GAUGE
In Lace Pattern: 18 sts = 4 inches; 10 rows = 4 inches

Take time to check gauge.

PATTERN NOTES
Weave in loose ends as work progresses.

Chain-1 at beginning of row does not count as a stitch.

Chain-3 at beginning of row counts as first double crochet unless otherwise stated.

Join with slip stitch as indicated unless otherwise stated.

PATTERN STITCHES
Lace Pattern

Row 1 (WS): Ch 3 *(see Pattern Notes)*, dc in **front lp** *(see Stitch Guide)* of next sc, sk next sc, [(dc, ch 1, dc) in front lp of next sc, sk 2 sc] across to last 4 sts, (dc, ch 1, dc) in front lp of next sc, sk next sc, dc in front lp of last 2 sc, turn.

Row 2: Ch 1 *(see Pattern Notes)*, sc in first 2 dc, [sk next dc, 3 sc in next ch-1 sp, sk next dc] across to last 2 sts, sc in next dc, sc in top of beg ch-3, turn.

Rep [rows 1 and 2 alternately] for pattern.

Body Texture

Row 1 (WS): Ch 1 *(see Pattern Notes)*, sc in first st, ch 1, sk next sc, [sc in next sc, ch 1, sk next sc] across to last st, sc in last st, turn.

Row 2: Ch 1, sc in first sc, ch 1, sk next ch-1 sp, [sc in next sc, ch 1, sk next ch-1 sp] across to last sc, sc in last sc, turn.

Rep row 2 for pattern.

TEE
BACK
Yoke
Piece is worked from top down.

Row 1: Loosely ch 125 [134, 143, 152, 161, 170], work sc in 2nd ch from hook and in each ch across. *(124 [133, 142, 151, 160, 169] sc)*

Work **Lace Pattern** *(see Pattern Stitches)* until piece measures 5 [5½, 6, 6½, 7, 7½] inches, ending with a WS row.

Next row (RS): Ch 1, sc in first 2 dc, [sk next dc, 3 sc in next ch-1 sp, sk next dc] across to last (dc, ch 1, dc), sk next dc, 2 [3, 2, 3, 2, 3] sc in last ch-1 sp, sk next dc, sc in next dc, sc in top of beg ch-3, turn. *(123 [133, 141, 151, 159, 169] sc)*

Continue in **Body Texture** *(see Pattern Stitches)* until piece measures 7 [7½, 8, 8½, 9, 9½] inches, ending with a WS row.

Fasten off.

Body
Row 1 (RS): Sk first 18 sts, **join** *(see Pattern Notes)* yarn in next sc, ch 1, sc in same st, ch 1, sk next ch-1 sp, [sc in next sc, ch 1, sk next ch-1 sp] across to last 19 sts, sc in next sc, turn, leaving rem 18 sts unworked. *(87 [97, 105, 115, 123, 133] sts)*

Continue in established Body Texture until piece measures approximately 14 [15½, 16, 16½, 17, 17½] inches from armhole *(22 [23, 24, 25, 26, 27] inches total)*.

Fasten off.

FRONT
Yoke
Piece is worked from top down, working each shoulder separately and then joining at front neckline and working down as on back piece.

Right Shoulder
Row 1 (RS): Holding back piece with RS facing, join yarn in first foundation

ch in upper right corner, ch 1, sc in same st, sc in next 45 [48, 51, 57, 60, 66] foundation chs, turn. *(46 [49, 52, 58, 61, 67] sc)*

Row 2: Ch 3, dc in front lp of next sc, sk next sc, [(dc, ch 1, dc) in front lp of next sc, sk 2 sc] across to last 4 sts, (dc, ch 1, dc) in front lp of next sc, sk next sc, dc in front lp of last 2 sc, turn.

Row 3: Ch 1, sc in first 2 dc, [sk next dc, 3 sc in next ch-1 sp, sk next dc] across to last 2 sts, sc in next dc, sc in top of beg ch-3, turn.

Row 4: Rep row 2.

Row 5: Ch 1, sc in first 2 dc, [sk next dc, 3 sc in next ch-1 sp, sk next dc] across to last 2 sts, sc in next dc, 2 sc in top of beg ch-3, turn. *(47 [50, 53, 59, 62, 68] sc)*

Row 6: Ch 3, dc in front lp of same sc, [(dc, ch 1, dc) in front lp of next sc, sk 2 sc] across to last 4 sts, (dc, ch 1, dc) in front lp of next sc, sk next sc, dc in front lp of last 2 sc, turn.

Row 7: Rep row 5. *(50 [53, 56, 62, 65, 71] sc)*

Fasten off.

Left Shoulder

Row 1 (RS): Sk next 32 [35, 38, 35, 38, 35] foundation chs on back piece and join yarn in next ch, ch 1, sc in same st and in rem 45 [48, 51, 57, 60, 66] foundation chs, turn. *(46 [49, 52, 58, 61, 67] sc)*

Row 2: Ch 3, dc in front lp of next sc, sk next sc, [(dc, ch 1, dc) in front lp of next sc, sk 2 sc] across to last 4 sts, (dc, ch 1, dc) in front lp of next sc, sk next sc, dc in front lp of last 2 sc, turn.

Row 3: Ch 1, sc in first 2 dc, [sk next dc, 3 sc in next ch-1 sp, sk next dc] across to last 2 sts, sc in next dc, sc in top of beg ch-3, turn.

Row 4: Rep row 2.

Row 5: Ch 1, 2 sc in first dc, sc in next dc, [sk next dc, 3 sc in next ch-1 sp, sk next dc] across to last 2 sts, sc in next dc, sc in top of beg ch-3, turn. *(47 [50, 53, 59, 62, 68] sc)*

Row 6: Ch 3, dc in front lp of same sc, sk next sc, [(dc, ch 1, dc) in front lp of next sc, sk 2 sc] across to last 5 sts, (dc, ch 1, dc) in front lp of next sc, sk next 2 sc, (dc, ch 1, dc) in front lp of next sc, 2 dc in front lp of last sc, turn.

Row 7: Rep row 5. *(50 [53, 56, 62, 65, 71] sc)*

Neckline Joining

Row 8 (WS): Ch 3, dc in front lp of same sc, sk next sc, [(dc, ch 1, dc) in front lp of next sc, sk 2 sc] across to last 5 sts, (dc, ch 1, dc) in front lp of next sc, sk next 2 sc, (dc, ch 1, dc) in front lp of next sc, 2 dc in front lp of last sc, ch 20 [23, 26, 23, 26, 23] *(ch-band)*, 2 dc in front lp of first sc on Right Shoulder, [(dc, ch 1, dc) in front lp of next sc, sk 2 sc] across to last 4 sts, (dc, ch 1, dc) in front lp of next sc, sk next sc, dc in front lp of last 2 sc, turn.

Row 9: Ch 1, sc in first 2 dc, [sk next dc, 3 sc in next ch-1 sp, sk next dc] across to last 2 dc before ch-band, sc in next 2 dc, sc in next 20 [23, 26, 23, 26, 23] chs, sc in next 2 dc, [sk next dc, 3 sc in next ch-1 sp, sk next dc] across to last 2 sts, sc in next dc, sc in top of beg ch-3, turn. *(124 [133, 142, 151, 160, 169] sc)*

Continue in established Lace Pattern until piece measures 5 [5½, 6, 6½, 7, 7½] inches, measured from top of shoulder, ending with a WS row.

Next row (RS): Ch 1, sc in first 2 dc, [sk next dc, 3 sc in next ch-1 sp, sk next dc] across to last (dc, ch 1, dc), sk next dc, 2 [3, 2, 3, 2, 3] sc in last ch-1 sp, sk next dc, sc in next dc, sc in top of beg ch-3, turn. *(123 [133, 141, 151, 159, 169] sc)*

Continue in Body Texture pattern until piece measures 7 [7½, 8, 8½, 9, 9½] inches, ending with a WS row.

Fasten off.

BODY

Work as for Back to same measurement.

Fasten off.

ASSEMBLY

Starting at sleeve edge, sew under sleeve seam to armhole, then continue with side seam from armhole and down, leaving a 4-inch split at bottom of side. Rep on other side.

FINISHING

Weave in ends. Block to measurements. ●

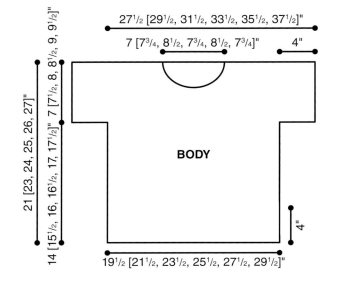

27½ [29½, 31½, 33½, 35½, 37½]"

7 [7¾, 8½, 7¾, 8½, 7¾]"   4"

21 [23, 24, 25, 26, 27]"

7 [7½, 8, 8½, 9, 9½]"

14 [15½, 16, 16½, 17, 17½]"

4"

BODY

4"

19½ [21½, 23½, 25½, 27½, 29½]"

STITCH GUIDE

STITCH ABBREVIATIONS

beg .... begin/begins/beginning
bpdc .... back post double crochet
bpsc ....back post single crochet
bptr ....back post treble crochet
CC .... contrasting color
ch(s) ....chain(s)
ch- .... refers to chain or space
previously made (i.e., ch-1 space)
ch sp(s) .... chain space(s)
cl(s) .... cluster(s)
cm .... centimeter(s)
dc ....double crochet (singular/plural)
dc dec .... double crochet 2 or more
stitches together, as indicated
dec ....decrease/decreases/decreasing
dtr .... double treble crochet
ext ....extended
fpdc .... front post double crochet
fpsc .... front post single crochet
fptr .... front post treble crochet
g ....gram(s)
hdc .... half double crochet
hdc dec .... half double crochet 2 or more
stitches together, as indicated
inc ....increase/increases/increasing
lp(s) .... loop(s)
MC .... main color
mm .... millimeter(s)
oz .... ounce(s)
pc .... popcorn(s)
rem .... remain/remains/remaining
rep(s) ....repeat(s)
rnd(s) ....round(s)
RS .... right side(s)
sc ....single crochet (singular/plural)
sc dec ....single crochet 2 or more
stitches together, as indicated
sk .... skip/skipped/skipping
sl st(s) ....slip stitch(es)
sp(s) .... space(s)/spaced
st(s) ....stitch(es)
tog ....together
tr. .... treble crochet
trtr .... triple treble
WS .... wrong side(s)
yd(s) .... yard(s)
yo .... yarn over

YARN CONVERSION

OUNCES TO GRAMS	GRAMS TO OUNCES
1 .... 28.4	25 ....⅞
2 .... 56.7	40 .... 1⅔
3 .... 85.0	50 .... 1¾
4 .... 113.4	100 .... 3½

UNITED STATES		UNITED KINGDOM
sl st (slip stitch)	=	sc (single crochet)
sc (single crochet)	=	dc (double crochet)
hdc (half double crochet)	=	htr (half treble crochet)
dc (double crochet)	=	tr (treble crochet)
tr (treble crochet)	=	dtr (double treble crochet)
dtr (double treble crochet)	=	ttr (triple treble crochet)
skip	=	miss

Single crochet decrease (sc dec): (Insert hook, yo, draw lp through) in each of the sts indicated, yo, draw through all lps on hook.

Example of 2-sc dec

Half double crochet decrease (hdc dec): (Yo, insert hook, yo, draw lp through) in each of the sts indicated, yo, draw through all lps on hook.

Example of 2-hdc dec

Reverse single crochet (reverse sc): Ch 1, sk first st, working from left to right, insert hook in next st from front to back, draw up lp on hook, yo and draw through both lps on hook.

Chain (ch): Yo, pull through lp on hook.

Single crochet (sc): Insert hook in st, yo, pull through st, yo, pull through both lps on hook.

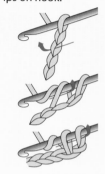

Double crochet (dc): Yo, insert hook in st, yo, pull through st, [yo, pull through 2 lps] twice.

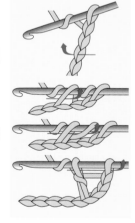

Double crochet decrease (dc dec): (Yo, insert hook, yo, draw lp through, yo, draw through 2 lps on hook) in each of the sts indicated, yo, draw through all lps on hook.

Example of 2-dc dec

Front loop (front lp): Back loop (back lp):

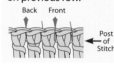

Front Loop   Back Loop

Front post stitch (fp): Back post stitch (bp): When working post st, insert hook from right to left around post of st on previous row.

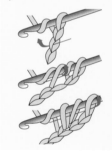

Back   Front

Post of Stitch →

Half double crochet (hdc): Yo, insert hook in st, yo, pull through st, yo, pull through all 3 lps on hook.

Double treble crochet (dtr): Yo 3 times, insert hook in st, yo, pull through st, [yo, pull through 2 lps] 4 times.

Treble crochet decrease (tr dec): Holding back last lp of each st, tr in each of the sts indicated, yo, pull through all lps on hook.

Example of 2-tr dec

Slip stitch (sl st): Insert hook in st, pull through both lps on hook.

Chain color change (ch color change): Yo with new color, draw through last lp on hook.

Double crochet color change (dc color change): Drop first color, yo with new color, draw through last 2 lps of st.

Treble crochet (tr): Yo twice, insert hook in st, yo, pull through st, [yo, pull through 2 lps] 3 times.

Metric Conversion Charts

METRIC CONVERSIONS

yards	x	.9144	=	meters (m)
yards	x	91.44	=	centimeters (cm)
inches	x	2.54	=	centimeters (cm)
inches	x	25.40	=	millimeters (mm)
inches	x	.0254	=	meters (m)

centimeters	x	.3937	=	inches
meters	x	1.0936	=	yards

INCHES INTO MILLIMETRES & CENTIMETRES (Rounded off slightly)

inches	mm	cm	inches	cm	inches	cm	inches	cm
1/8	3	0.3	5	12.5	21	53.5	38	96.5
1/4	6	0.6	5 1/2	14	22	56	39	99
3/8	10	1	6	15	23	58.5	40	101.5
1/2	13	1.3	7	18	24	61	41	104
5/8	15	1.5	8	20.5	25	63.5	42	106.5
3/4	20	2	9	23	26	66	43	109
7/8	22	2.2	10	25.5	27	68.5	44	112
1	25	2.5	11	28	28	71	45	114.5
1 1/4	32	3.2	12	30.5	29	73.5	46	117
1 1/2	38	3.8	13	33	30	76	47	119.5
1 3/4	45	4.5	14	35.5	31	79	48	122
2	50	5	15	38	32	81.5	49	124.5
2 1/2	65	6.5	16	40.5	33	84	50	127
3	75	7.5	17	43	34	86.5		
3 1/2	90	9	18	46	35	89		
4	100	10	19	48.5	36	91.5		
4 1/2	115	11.5	20	51	37	94		

KNITTING NEEDLES CONVERSION CHART

Canada/U.S.	0	1	2	3	4	5	6	7	8	9	10	10½	11	13	15
Metric (mm)	2	2¼	2¾	3¼	3½	3¾	4	4½	5	5½	6	6½	8	9	10

CROCHET HOOKS CONVERSION CHART

Canada/U.S.	1/B	2/C	3/D	4/E	5/F	6/G	7	8/H	9/I	10/J	10½/K	N
Metric (mm)	2.25	2.75	3.25	3.5	3.75	4	4.5	5	5.5	6	6.5	9.0

Published by Annie's, 306 East Parr Road, Berne, IN 46711. Printed in USA. Copyright © 2024 Annie's. All rights reserved. This publication may not be reproduced in part or in whole without written permission from the publisher.

RETAIL STORES: If you would like to carry this publication or any other Annie's publication, visit AnniesWSL.com.

Every effort has been made to ensure that the instructions in this publication are complete and accurate. We cannot, however, take responsibility for human error, typographical mistakes or variations in individual work. Please visit AnniesCustomerService.com to check for pattern updates.

ISBN: 979-8-89253-381-2

1 2 3 4 5 6 7 8 9